IMAGES of America
THE ROYCROFT CAMPUS

THE ROYCROFT CAMPUS

IMAGES of America

Robert Rust and Kitty Turgeon

Copyright © 1999, 2000 by Robert Rust and Kitty Turgeon.
ISBN 0-7524-1344-9

First printed 1999.

Published by Arcadia Publishing,
an imprint of Tempus Publishing, Inc.
2 Cumberland Street
Charleston, SC 29401

Printed in Great Britain.

Library of Congress Catalog Card Number: 99-61842

For all general information contact Arcadia Publishing at:
Telephone 843-853-2070
Fax 843-853-0044
E-Mail sales@arcadiapublishing.com

For customer service and orders:
Toll-Free 1-888-313-2665

Visit us on the internet at http://www.arcadiaimages.com

To All the Roycrofters Past and Present

This book could not have been completed in only a year without the word processing and layout help of the Foundation's Assistant Director, Tisha Zawisky. We really appreciate the cooperation, understanding, and friendly assistance of Arcadia's editors, who made writing this book an enjoyable project.

Contents

	Introduction	7
1.	Elbert Hubbard and Family	9
2.	The Roycroft Shops	27
3.	The Roycroft Inn	45
4.	Roycroft Artisans and Workers	69
5.	Visitors to the Campus and What They Saw	89
6.	Objects Made by Roycrofters	105
7.	The Roycroft Renaissance	115

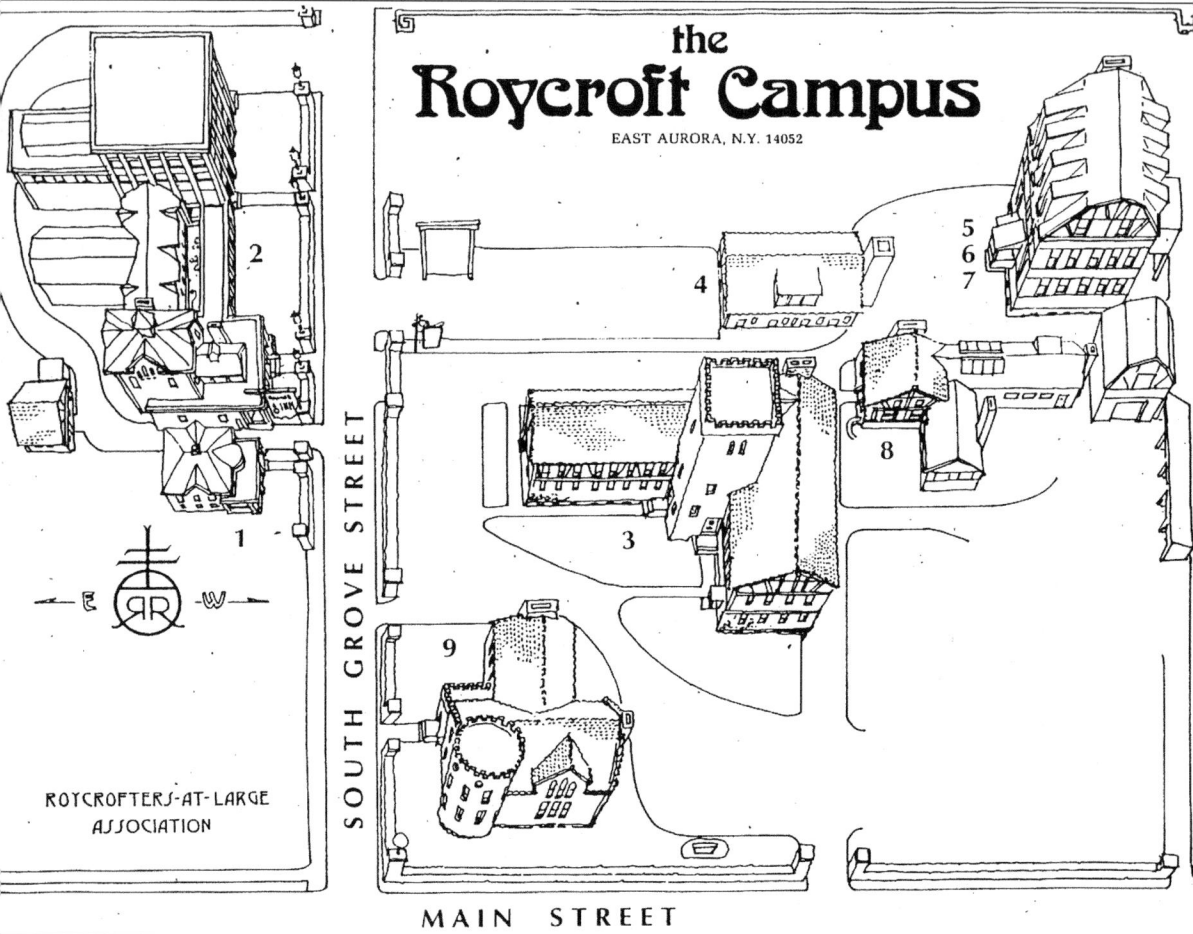

Rixford Jennings, one of the founders of Roycrofters At Large Association (RALA) and the artisan to span both eras, made this aerial view of the campus in the early 1980s. It has been used in various publications ever since. The historic and current use of each building is listed below.

HISTORIC, C. 1912
1. Special Guesthouse
2. Roycroft Inn
3. Print Shop
4. Power House
5. Furniture Shop
6. Bindery
7. Leather Shop
8. Copper Shop

9. Chapel, Library, Art Gallery

TODAY, C. 2000
1. Hotel rooms
2. Roycroft Inn
3. Cornell Extension Center
4. Saved after fire; renovation in progress
5. Roycroft Antiques; Hubbard's Cupboard
6. Roycroft Potters
7. Norberg's Art Gallery
8. Roycroft Shops & 2/R Fine Art Gallery
   Foundation for the Study of the Arts & Crafts Movement at Roycroft
9. Aurora Town Hall and Museum

INTRODUCTION

Roycroft is as much a state of mind as a place; this paraphrases what Elbert Hubbard had in mind when he founded the utopian craft community more than 100 years ago. The first Roycroft publication was printed in 1895.

Originally devoted to the making of beautiful books in the manner of William Morris, the Roycrofters soon developed a wide range of arts and crafts items for sale. What they made to furnish and decorate their expanding Roycroft Campus was soon being sold by catalog.

The unique combination of the Hubbard family, artisans, and workers created a multi-level complex operation that included books, art, education, music, and magazines.

This book explores the key factors that made the Roycroft Campus a fascinating social experiment and made it eligible for National Historic Landmark status. That designation was given in March 1986.

We have been collecting Roycroft memorabilia in many forms for more than 25 years. The historic photographs are of particular interest to Robert, who studied photography at Visual Studies Workshop in Rochester, New York. We both have degrees in historic preservation and have made more than a career at Roycroft during what is known as the Roycroft Renaissance. We are the founders and directors of two not-for-profit organizations dedicated to the Arts & Crafts (A&C) Movement history, its revival, and to Roycroft.

All of the photographs are from our private collection, and we are eager and proud to share them in this book. Many have never before been published; some have not been seen in 75 years. A number of them have been displayed in various A&C and Roycroft exhibitions that have travelled around the country. Our own turn-of-the-century 2/R Fine Arts Gallery has exhibited many of these photographs over the past 10 years.

First, we will cover the man who loved to be photographed, Elbert Greene Hubbard. He appears in a number of portraits made by famous photographers. His two wives and five children, as well as their children, are the subjects of several more images.

Architecture is a key element of the Roycroft Campus. Roycroft Shop buildings and the Roycroft Inn were subjects substantially recorded by the Roycrofters as a means of promotion in their brochures, postcards, catalogues, and magazines. Fortunately, we have a wealth of that material.

Chapter Three focuses on the Roycroft Inn, which we owned and operated for some time, beginning in 1971. It has recently been restored (1995) and reopened by the Margaret L. Wendt Foundation. We feel fortunate to have been able to sell the Roycroft Inn to a non-profit organization that could put $8 million into its marvelous renovation.

The artisans and workers, talented and dedicated individuals, were the subject of photographs taken on numerous occasions. We included both formal and casual shots of all.

We will explore the village of East Aurora, both its historic Main Street and the houses that were built or used by the Roycrofters for living and working. We have included some of their outdoor activities, including farming and playing.

The main craft at Roycroft was printing books and magazines. Fine copper, furniture, and leather goods were promoted and sold primarily by the catalogues the Roycrofters printed. Reprints of examples are included in this publication.

Postcards were printed during the four decades of the original Roycroft Campus, and their inclusion through most of the chapters is a valuable addition. Some cards were hand-colored; later ones were printed in color. The black-and-white renditions here require your imagination.

A succession of art directors at Roycroft reflects changing styles and tastes. Early Morrisian English A&C designs by Samuel Warner at Roycroft (1898–1902) set the initial tone. From 1904 to 1910, Dard Hunter's exceedingly modern, Vienna Secession-style book frontispieces and motto borders provided a new look. The Roycroft enterprise had many artists, and a wealth of graphic art inspiration spread from East Aurora around the world.

Hubbard was the paternalistic leader of a corporation that was determined to make a profit. The community was a congenial group who held stock in the corporation, banked at the Elbert Hubbard Bank, and played music and sports together. Many lived in houses built by their fellow workers. Roycroft was never a commune; the Roycroft Campus was a unique school and definitely a place of learning. Courses were taught formally as an extra-curricular activity for workers who followed the apprentice system.

We have attempted to put each chapter's photographs in chronological order. Two maps, one of the campus and the other showing East Aurora's location in western New York, will further our goal of a simple and interesting history.

The A&C lifestyle, as practiced by Hubbard and his Roycrofters, was promoted by his lectures and in the locally printed magazines. Roycroft soon became a household name.

Alice and Elbert Hubbard were tragically lost at sea in the sinking of the *Lusitania*. Bert (Elbert II) Hubbard carried on very well until the Great Depression, and the Roycroft Campus went out of business in 1938. Elbert Hubbard's memory grew dim until recently. We hope this publication will help to restore the fame of his name and that of the Roycroft Campus.

One
Elbert Hubbard and Family

Elbert Greene Hubbard was born June 19, 1856, the third child to a country doctor and his wife in Bloomington, Illinois. His parents had moved west after their sojourn in western New York on the Seneca Indian Reservation. Dr. Silas was from a large family from Mayville, New York, on Chatauqua Lake. Juliana Reed Hubbard, a young teacher, was from Buffalo, the daughter of a bookbinder. Elbert's father was a phrenologist, having studied medicine at Castleton College in Vermont. Apparently, he was a good doctor who never earned much money because he often gave away his services.

With little formal schooling, Elbert Hubbard went to work selling soap for a cousin in Chicago. He married Bertha Crawford in 1879. They moved to Buffalo, where Elbert joined his sister Frances's husband, John Larkin, as a partner in the Larkin Co., another soap business. In 1883, the young Hubbard and their son Bert moved to East Aurora, New York, and for ten years he commuted by train to work in Buffalo.

His liaison with Alice Moore began in the late 1880s; she soon encouraged his writing and subsequent "dropping out" of the "establishment" or traditional world. After a six-week stint at Harvard, he traveled to England to research his *Little Journeys to the Homes of the Great,* soon to be published by J.P. Putnam & Sons. A daughter, Miriam, was born to Elbert and Alice in 1894, and only a year later, Katherine was born to he and his wife, Bertha. The man was torn between his respect and love for the two women, but divorce and remarriage was the eventual result between 1902 and 1904.

Elbert Hubbard founded the Roycroft Press in 1895, and two years later, he began building what was to become the Roycroft Campus. The success of his essay "A Message to Garcia" (1899) catapulted him and the Roycroft to fame and enough fortune to build his Roycroft Campus bigger and better and, eventually, to employ nearly 500 people.

After Alice and Elbert's death on the *Lusitania* in 1915, Elbert II (Bert) and his wife, Alta, ran the enterprise differently, but with a financial stability that was better than ever through the 1920s. Changing tastes and, especially, the Great Depression, dragged the Roycrofters into bankruptcy by 1938. Bert and Alta lived on as prominent citizens of East Aurora; he even served as mayor. Their children stayed in the area. Their only son, Elbert Hubbard III (known as John), became a doctor; he is now retired. Their youngest daughter, Nancy Hubbard Brady, was one of the founders of the RALA; she died in 1982. Her daughter Linda carries on the book business, "The House of Hubbard." Miriam's six children dispersed to several places around the East Coast. Her eldest daughter, Mary Roelofs Stott, became a noted author and musician; there is an award fund in her name. One of the Hubbard's farms, the Arden Farm, is still in Miriam's family; run by her youngest son, Mark, it provides organic produce for the western New York community.

In 1873, at age 17, Elbert is already a young traveling salesman. His formal education is complete and he is studying on his own. He holds a good job as a salesman working for Justus Weller, his cousin, in the Chicago-based Weller Soap Company.

Elbert Hubbard, a the young successful businessman, is shown here in 1882 at age 26. After only seven years in partnership with his brother-in-law, John D. Larkin, he was made a junior partner, sales manager, and vice president. Hubbard's corporate acumen and advertising genius in the Larkin Soap Company made him invaluable. Two years later, he and his wife, Bertha Crawford, and their young son Bert (Elbert Hubbard II) moved to East Aurora, 16 miles from Buffalo. He commuted to the city and the Larkin Enterprise while enjoying the country life with horses that the small village has as its claim to fame.

Hubbard has refined his image; now an author of several articles for Boston literary magazines, he decides to sell out his interest in the Larkin Company to his brother-in-law. Due to an economic recession, his poor timing nets him only about $75,000 in this transaction. His intention is to enroll as a special student at Harvard, which he does in spring 1893.

Fit and handsome, Elbert Hubbard has recently returned from his 1894 tour of Europe, where he prepared for his upcoming series of biographical essays on famous people. They are titled *Little Journeys to the Homes of the Great*, published by G.P. Putnam. His relationship with Alice Moore, a native of nearby Wales Hollow, New York, whom he had met in East Aurora (where she was the preceptress of the local school), ignited when she was a boarder in the Hubbard home. Their liaison continued in Concord, Massachusetts, where they lived as a married couple for a brief time. In September of 1894, she gave birth to their daughter, Miriam. Elbert founded the Roycroft Press in East Aurora the following year.

This is the premiere issue (June 1895) of *The Philistine* magazine, a "Periodical of Protest." Elbert joins forces with a local journalist and salesman Harry P. Taber to publish under the aegis of the "Roycroft Printing Shop." Within a year, Hubbard buys out his partner and assumes complete control of the publication.

A proud father poses with two of his three sons. On the left, Elbert Hubbard II (Bert) (1882-1970), who has already traveled to Britain and visited William Morris's Kelmscott Press with his dad in 1896. On the right is his second son, Ralph (1885–1980). In 1898, he followed his brother on Elbert's third trip to Europe to conduct further research on *Little Journeys*. The series continued for 14 years, one journey each month. Every year a different category was chosen, starting with English authors, continuing on with famous teachers, poets, philosophers, musicians, artists, women, and lovers, etc., and ending with great businessmen.

In the Oak Room, later the library, of the first print shop, this c. 1899 photo of Alta Fattey (left) and Bertha Crawford Hubbard (right) shows the two women practicing mineral art or china painting. This hobby led both of them to become the early illuminators for the Roycroft books. Bertha, in fact, was the designer of the first two Roycroft Press title pages for *Song of Songs* (1896) and *The Journal of Koheleth* (1897), both written by her husband, Elbert Hubbard. Alta was to marry Bert (Elbert Hubbard II), and they ran the Roycroft Inn and Shops, following the death of his father and stepmother.

The Roycroft woodpile was an exercise that was encouraged for Roycrofters and guests alike. One of Elbert's sons demonstrates this fine technique on Roycroft fitness equipment—the two-hand saw. In the background is the newly built second print shop and the foundation for the blacksmith (later the copper shop), which was completed that year. This picture was taken c. 1902.

Fra Elbertus is shown in his favorite persona—flowing Byron tie, Stetson hat, homespun suit, long hair, and serious stance. He was the leader of the Arts & Crafts Movement. This photo was used to promote and advertise his many lectures across the United States. The signed photograph is one of the many hundreds that Elbert sat for. Like a movie star, he would autograph pictures of himself.

Elbert Hubbard not only invented the premium method of merchandising, but also the "personal endorsement" to promote products as far reaching as automobiles, breakfast cereal, chewing gum and, as seen here, elegant summer suits. Many of the ads were featured in the monthly *Fra* magazine, which had a circulation of almost 100,000 per month from 1908 to 1917.

This picture, one of the most prominent images by the famous Chicago portrait photographer Moffet, shows Elbert Hubbard and his true love and second wife, Alice Moore Hubbard. Growing from their mutual intellectual respect, they found themselves devoted to a common ideal and soon a passionate relationship. They married in February 1904 after a long love affair. Alice, like Elbert's first wife, Bertha, was highly educated and every bit as intellectual as the charismatic Elbert Hubbard. They seemed destined for one another and together they epitomized the Roycroft.

A lithograph of Alice Hubbard and their daughter, Miriam, portrays the closeness of mother and daughter. Alice advocated in her book *Life Lessons* (from which this image originates) that the state should support mothers who were responsible for the future of the country. Alice was a strong suffragette, insisting her husband put a sign on one of the Roycroft silos advocating "Votes for Women" in 2-foot-high letters.

"Elbert Hubbard and the Little Deluxe" (1900) shows Hubbard and his youngest child, Katherine, who was born to he and Bertha in January 1896. At only four years of age, she was featured in the catalog of Roycroft products. She grew up in Buffalo with her mother after her parents' divorce in 1903. She never married but became a school teacher in Washington, D.C., and was never again involved in the Roycroft. She lived with her mother and always remained loyal to her. Bertha passed away in 1946; Katherine died in 1961.

In this scene from the winter of 1910, Elbert Hubbard is shown astride "Garnet," his mare. They are accompanied by her colt, who was called "Asbestos" because "he was such hot stuff" (as noted on the back of the photograph). The caption on back also states that Elbert was on his way from the Roycroft Stable to visit his parents, who had recently moved to East Aurora. The senior Hubbards lived only a block from the Roycroft Campus.

The whole family enjoys their favorite pastime on South Grove Street in front of the Roycroft Inn, c. 1909. Alice is astride "Babe," Elbert is on his famous "Garnet," and Miriam rides her own special horse.

This c. 1910 photo captures a scene of mother and son. Dr. Silas Hubbard (1821–1917) and Juliana Hubbard (1829–1924), the parents of Elbert Hubbard, moved to East Aurora after retiring; they lived around the corner from the Roycroft Campus and were much involved in the community of Roycrofters before and after their son's death.

Alice Moore Hubbard, the serene chatelaine of the Roycroft Campus in 1914, ran the Roycroft Inn and Shops with strength and vision for ten years. She authored four books and numerous articles printed at Roycroft. Some of the artisans had trouble with a woman in charge; some left and some grudgingly stayed. Emil Sahlin, a young printer who died in 1988, remembered that "You could hear the rustle of her taffeta skirt and everyone stepped up the pace and paid attention."

A noted woman pictorialist and member of the Alfred Stieglitz inner circle, Elizabeth "Bessie" Bheurman (exact spelling of surname unknown) of Chicago was a visitor at the Roycroft Campus, where she took this rare and revealing platinum photograph of Hubbard. The almost 20 years of patriarchy of the Roycroft Campus and the responsibility of a payroll for almost 500 workers was enormous. Signs of fame and stress are evident.

Ready for sailing, this photograph by Henry Lee of Alice and Elbert Hubbard was taken on the pier awaiting the sailing of the S.S. *Lusitania* on May 1, 1915, in New York City. He had assembled his Roycrofters together only the day before in the music salon of the Roycroft Inn to discuss their upcoming trip to Europe. His hope was to meet with the Kaiser in Germany to plead for the cause of peace. Alice had persuaded Elbert to include her on the trip, despite all the warnings in New York City newspapers by the German government that had threatened the ship by its U-boat fleet.

This is the final photograph of the Fra on the deck of the Cunard's *Lusitania* on May 1, 1915. Just before the ship set sail, a photographer named Bain recorded the flamboyant pacifist, editor, writer, and publisher as he faced his final mission.

This solemn occasion is the memorial procession of the over 2,000 people paying tribute to the memory of Alice and Elbert Hubbard. The large gathering marched from Main Street, East Aurora, down South Grove Street past the Roycroft Inn, where this photo was taken. The procession ended at the Roycroft Pavilion in Hamlin Park, where the services were held.

Two riderless horses, Babe and Garnet (Alice and Elbert's favorite mares), with boots in backwards, represented their owners in a solemn parade to honor the two lost at sea. All of the family members, except for son Ralph, who was at school in Colorado, attended the service. Bertha Crawford Hubbard (1861–1935) was one of several to eulogize the departed.

This 1914 photograph shows Miriam Hubbard at the Roycroft Well Sweep, just off the Appian Way. The picturesque location was a favorite site for photographers and visitors. C.H. Kingsbury of Buffalo took this charming picture of the college schoolgirl after her sophomore year at the University of Michigan.

Before leaving to sail on the *Lusitania*, Elbert Hubbard called his beloved Roycrofters together to say goodbye and said that if he didn't return (the ship had been threatened by the Germans), Bert (Elbert Hubbard II) would be in charge and run the Roycroft Inn and Shops. This 1915 photograph showing the new president of the Roycrofters, Inc., was used to announce his leadership. Bert left school at age 15 to work in the family business. Little did he know that, at age 33, he would assume command of a national concern, the village's largest enterprise.

Elbert Hubbard II was a handsome "sage in a sage's shadow" according to Charlie Hamilton, his biographer. In 1916, a year after his father's death, he arranged a contract with a New York City publishing firm, Wm. Wise & Co., to have the Roycrofters print a 14-volume set of *Little Journeys*. The undertaking provided employment and profit for the Roycrofters into the 1920s. Tens of thousands of sets were sold throughout the world. This image is by noted "Photographer of Men" Perie MacDonald of New York, c. 1920.

Grandfather and Grandmother Hubbard, a tryptic from the *Fra* magazine of 1916, shows Dr. Silas Hubbard (1821–1917) and Juliana Frances Reed Hubbard (1829–1924). They were married in 1849. Around their 50th anniversary, they relocated to this home on Oakwood Avenue, around the corner from their son's Roycroft Campus. Silas became the Roycroft doctor in his retirement, often challenging his son during his Sunday night lectures in the Roycroft Inn's Music Salon.

Shown here "sitting for a portrait" is Nancy Hubbard at less than two years of age. A latecomer to the Roycroft Campus, a friend of Alex Fournier, and a native of Hungary, Sandor Landeau is seen in the Fournier backyard outside the "Bunglehouse," painting the child while Emma Fournier and Alta Hubbard, Nancy's mother, look on. The oil canvas created at this sitting is still in the family.

This is a family portrait of Sanford (Sandy) Hubbard, the youngest son of Elbert and Bertha Hubbard, with his wife, Georgiana, and their son Silas. Sandy was noted throughout the nation for his activities with the Boy Scouts. He was also renowned as a builder of log cabins and log furniture. Many of his cabins still stand in western New York. He homesteaded with his bride on 640 acres in St. Joe, Idaho, in 1912. They returned to East Aurora in 1916, where they lived until he died in 1955. Georgiana lived until 1986, and Silas died in 1994. The photograph is by Francis Sipprell.

This 1916 image is titled "Planting the Memorial Tree." The tree was located on the Roycroft Campus grounds, across from the inn and just south of the Appian Way. Bert Hubbard is shown watering the tree, which had just been planted in memory of his father and Alice.

On June 19, 1930, a statue was unveiled to the memory of Elbert Hubbard on the Roycroft Campus at East Aurora, New York. Pictured from left to right are Elbert Hubbard III, Elbert Hubbard II, and sculptor Jerome Connor. Money was raised from subscribers throughout the nation to erect a fitting tribute to the Fra. Originally located on the Print Shop lawn, facing South Grove, it is presently located on the middle school lawn across Main Street. Jerome Connor was contacted in Ireland in 1926 to sculpt a likeness of Elbert, who was his patron and friend. Connor worked at the Roycroft from 1899, helping build the original buildings, as well as creating sculptures (several of Elbert), designing books, and working in wrought iron. He left to head up the metalwork department in Syracuse for Gustav Stickley's Craftsman Workshops in 1902.

The fountain in the courtyard garden of the Roycroft Inn attracts the attention of Bert and Alta Hubbard's three daughters. From left to right, they are Lynette (1906–), Nancy (1914–1982), and Elberta (1909–1970). This photograph was taken c. 1920 by Morrall.

In this 1977 view, four generations of Hubbard women pose in the William Morris Room of the Roycroft Inn. Miriam Hubbard Roelofs, the daughter of Elbert and Alice, is seated. On the right is Nancy Hubbard Brady, the granddaughter of Elbert and Bertha. Also pictured are her daughter Linda and her children, Cindy (left) and Kelly Lynn Falkosky (front right).

Two
THE ROYCROFT SHOPS

This chapter is a record of the west side of the South Grove Street Roycroft Campus and the buildings that comprise the original Roycroft Shops. Included is the large house across the street south of the Roycroft Inn, which also is in the National Historic Landmark designation. Starting at the west corner of Main and South Grove Streets in East Aurora, we look first at the Roycroft Chapel, one of the most beautiful and impressive structures; it presently houses the Aurora Town Hall. Besides being home to the Town Board, the largest room at the south end hosts the Aurora Historical Society and Roycrofters-at-Large Association (RALA) meetings. It is a museum of town history, and Elderhostel makes use of it as a classroom. Moving down the street is the second print shop, built after the success of Hubbard's "Message to Garcia," which catapulted the Roycroft into fame and fortune and required a larger facility. That building is now owned by a farmers' cooperative and houses the Cornell Extension Center for Erie County, which administers 4-H, seeing-eye dog training, and many soil and pond testing offices. Everything is designed to help the farming community in the surrounding area, which is largely dairy farms. Bert Hubbard said his father would have loved this new use of the building. Next in line is the blacksmith shop, which became the copper shop c. 1908 and Elbert Hubbard's bank; it has been a retail shop since the 1930s. It now houses Roycroft Shops Inc. The Roycroft Printing museum uses an original 1897 press and is being established by the Foundation (FSA&CM) at Roycroft.

The furniture shop, which eventually became the bindery building, is now a series of antique shops, an art gallery, and the Roycroft Potters. The last structure, the Roycroft Power House, was erected in 1909 and is awaiting restoration after a devastating fire in 1997.

A friend, neighbor, and fellow traveler of Hubbard was Dr. Arthur L. Mitchell. His house, located south of the inn, was later the home of Elbert Hubbard II and his wife, Alta Fattey, who had originally built a house on the corner of North Grove Street and Ridge Avenue.

Many structures had to be moved in order to erect the Roycroft Campus. The common practice of moving buildings is no longer as practical as it was before telephone wires and other utility services made the procedure difficult. Most of these homes, many of which still exist today, were moved to the southern section of the village.

The misconception that that the Roycroft Campus is outside of the village of East Aurora is common. It became and still is at the center of the community. Two fires in the last two decades and the changing ownership of each of the buildings is generally unknown. The public often perceives the campus as a single entity. A growing cooperation among the eight owners of the 14 buildings in the National Historic Landmark are making a unified appearance possible. In 1998, the village of East Aurora reactivated a preservation commission and all the Roycroft buildings were included in a local landmark district. Local level supervision has far more power to protect than does the more prestigious Department of the Interior's National Historic Landmark designation.

An idealized Roycroft Campus was painted by Alex Fournier c. 1912. He was called "the court painter of the Roycroft." Fournier saw the Roycroft through its most glorious years. He was hired in the summer of 1904 to be the art director of the Roycrofters; he lived in a bungalow at 46 Walnut Street that had been built by the Roycroft building team.

The art gallery was located in the chapel (south wing) by 1904. The antiquarian meaning of "chapel" is the guild hall of the printers. This edifice was constructed in 1899 of local glacial fieldstone and was the second structure built on the campus.

The stone building at the corner of Main and South Grove Streets was the principal sales room of the Roycrofters. In this c. 1903 photograph, the lower turret room housed the area where visitors could view the work of many artisans; it was called "the Rest Room." Prior to 1903, the space exhibited the sculptures of Jerome Connor, the fine art of Samuel Warner, and perhaps the Roycroft art pottery of Carl Ahrens and his cousin, Eleanor Douglas.

One of the main meeting halls of the Roycrofters (c. 1905), this room was known as the Art Gallery. Here, fine oil paintings by many well-known artists were featured. Above the fireplace is a suspected work by N.C. Wyeth that depicts Tom Sawyer and Huckleberry Finn on a raft. Flanking it, on the mantle, are two early Teco pottery vases. To the left is a hand-carved, gilded leather screen by Frederick Kranz and a sculpture by Jerome Connor. The large, oak benches are Roycroft-made and were later moved to the Music Salon. Many still exist today. The gas lamps were made in the adjacent blacksmith shop and date from 1899.

The largest room in the chapel became known as the "Sales Room" a few years later. This building held the editorial and art departments for the Roycroft printing enterprise. The Viennese-style, green-and-lavender stained-glass lanterns made in the copper shop have replaced the gas lamps, and Alex Fournier's art is displayed above the fireplace. This room is a showroom for copper and books, which are displayed on dark oak tables and counters made in the furniture shop. Everything is very "Roycroftie."

According to the caption on the back of this image, "Sheep pastured on the front lawn around the Chapel (for a week or so)." Though this photograph looks too idyllic, Alex Fournier only removed the fence from this view to make his famous oil painting, *Peace*, which traveled throughout the country as part of "Head, Heart, & Hand," a major traveling retrospective exhibition of the Roycroft, which opened in 1995 at Rochester's Memorial Art Gallery.

This photograph of the Roycroft Chapel was published in the Roycroft Catalog of 1900. It was taken by Francis Benjamin Johnson and shows a rare view of the first blacksmith shop on the campus. Jerome Connor and Peter Robarge worked in this wooden shed.

Thick plank walls are the interior fabric of the first blacksmith shop. Within these walls, the earliest craft (other than printing) found its way into the Roycroft catalogs. Hubbard remarked that "due to his need to furnish his expanding Roycroft Campus, he hired the local smithy and set him up as an attraction for the growing number of visitors."

In the midst of the quaint western New York village of East Aurora on South Grove Street, visitors discover a medieval structure made of stone. To acquire the material, Elbert Hubbard's handyman, Anson Blackman, known to the Roycrofters and the world as "Ali Baba," sat each morning at this corner, handing out the Fra's silver dollars to each local farmer who would deposit a wagonload of fieldstone. This wonderful building material, a nuisance to the plow, composed many of the buildings of Hubbard's dream.

In this winter scene from the late 1920s, we recognize the grand entrance at South Grove Street to the Roycroft Campus. Pairs of double stone columns with electric street lamps flanked the avenue to the entire Roycroft Campus. After the demise of the Roycrofters, the street was widened and the two outer columns were demolished.

After the closing of the Roycroft enterprise in 1938 and its subsequent purchase by publisher Samuel Guard, who also went bankrupt, it was sold to the Baptist Church of East Aurora. It remained a "chapel" in the religious sense until the mid-fifties, when it was converted to the Aurora Town Hall. In 1999, it remains in that capacity.

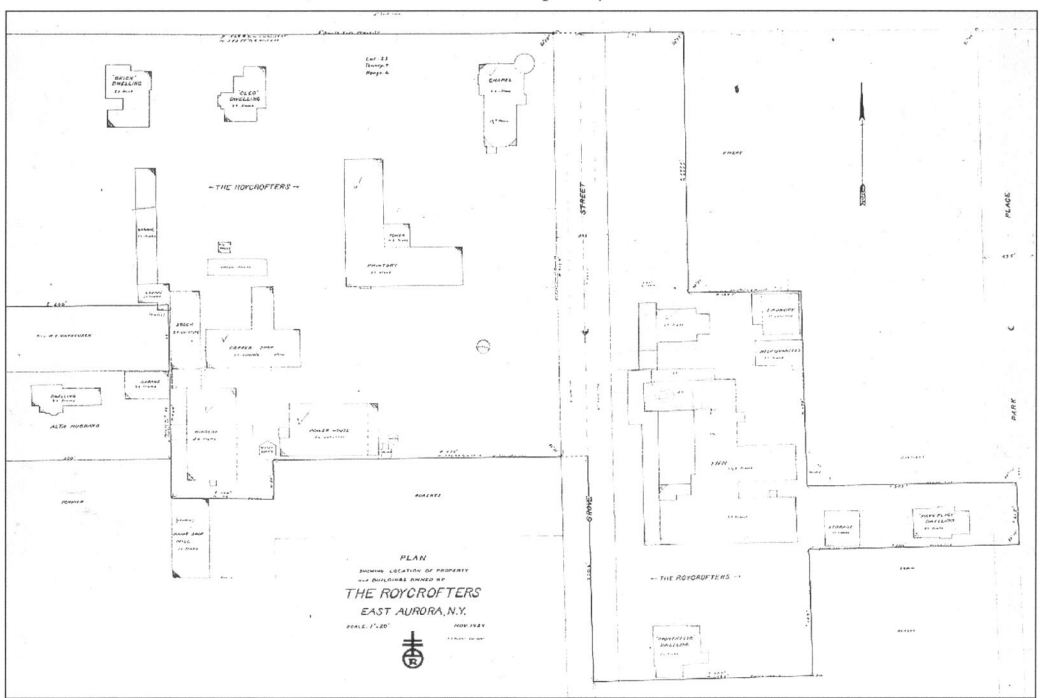

In this 1929 survey of the Roycrofters holdings on both sides of South Grove Street, over 18 buildings are shown spreading across the street, starting with the chapel in 1899 to include the second printery, 1900–1901; the copper shop, 1902; the bindery, also known as the furniture shop, 1904; and the power house, 1909–1910. Many existing homes were also under the Roycroft's ownership from Park Place at the east over to Walnut Street at the west.

Just south and slightly west of the new chapel, the Roycrofters built the second print shop. They needed this building due to the immense popularity of all things Roycroft, especially the March 1899 publishing of the "Message to Garcia." By the time this building opened in 1901, over 3 million copies of this 700-word essay had been printed. Elbert Hubbard had become a household name.

This typical western New York winter scene was photographed before 1905. The L-shaped, half-timbered-and-stone structure with its crenelated tower is reminiscent of the medieval buildings Hubbard saw on his travels in Britain. Over 200 workers were employed in the printing arts on three floors of the "new" print shop. According to the East Aurora *Advertiser* of February 21, 1901, "over 250 Roycrofters and guests attended the housewarming and dance."

The interior of what was known as "the ballroom" functions here for the collation of Roycroft books. The women were adept at this task, nicely dressed and of equal importance to the men who ran the presses in the cellars. Note that the Roycrofters made glass and wrought-iron chandeliers and wall sconces. These items were available for sale in the very first Roycroft Crafts Catalog of 1899–1900.

Handset type was the specialty of Roycroft printing. The composing room on the main floor, shown here, also housed the first Roycroft Press, which had been moved from the building across the street when it was converted into the Roycroft Inn. There it had been used to print the first *Philistine* magazines. Second from the left is typographer Emil George Sahlin, who came to the Roycroft in 1914, two years after his brother Axel joined the Roycrofters. They were both trained in Sweden. Starting in 1909, electricity and heat were provided for all the shops from the Roycroft's own power house.

On the lawn of the print shop, this wonderful sculpture of Michelangelo by Paul Bartlett (1865–1925) was installed facing east in 1908. Elbert Hubbard had commissioned this work after seeing a similar statue, which now stands on the grounds of the Library of Congress in Washington, D.C. It was then in the Capitol Building. In 1901, a model of this bronze sculpture won a gold medal at Buffalo's Pan American Exposition.

Directly across South Grove Street from the Roycroft Inn is the Appian Way, lined with trees and benches. Its entrance is marked by stone pillars, which at first were decorated with barrels of flowers. In front of the blacksmith shop stands the stone-sided well and well sweep, a favorite gathering place for the Roycrofters.

In this c. 1920 image of the print shop, taken from the southeast, we see a rare picture of the greenhouse to the north of the by-now-expanded copper shop. A unique box seat in a tree house offered a great view of the tennis and handball court to its left.

This is a rare view of Dr. Mitchell's house on South Grove Street. He was one of Elbert Hubbard's closest friends and a neighbor, and he traveled to Europe with him on two occasions. Next door, an unknown residence that no longer exists stood between the recently completed Roycroft Inn (c. 1904) and the Mitchell's home. Elbert Hubbard II (Bert) and Alta moved here as newlyweds. For a while, it was known as "Monticello."

Elbert Hubbard II, his wife, Alta, and their two young daughters, Lynette and Elberta, sit on the porch of their South Grove Street home, c. 1913, next door to the Roycroft Inn. Both houses were, at one time, owned by family friend Dr. Mitchell.

Built in 1904, this three-story wooden building with a full basement originally housed the furniture shop. Because of the cyclical nature of the furniture orders, this building also functioned as a bindery, for the main craft at Roycroft was the printing of books. From 1904 until 1910, it had its own generator producing the power for the many modern machines of the day. It should be noted that all of Roycroft's production was not exclusively done by hand.

Listed as a "Bench Floor in Furniture Shop" in the 1907 catalog, the main floor of the large, dormered wooden structure contained both hand-powered and electrical-powered equipment. Note the elevator in the center right of the photograph. Elbert's son Bert was superintendent of the shop in the early days. In this building, the furniture for their largest commission, the Grove Park Inn in Asheville, North Carolina, was built in 1912–1913.

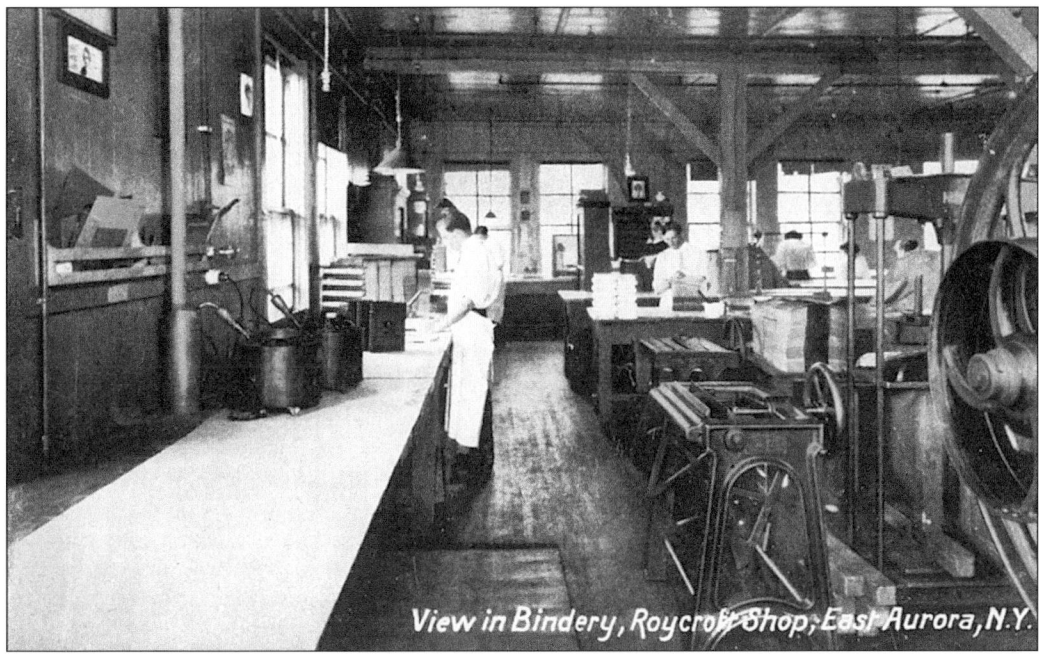

At the time of this c. 1905 photograph, the bindery was located on the second floor. Charles Youngers was the superintendent of the department. Master craftsman Louis Kinder had his fine leather binders at work on the third floor, where in earlier years, the furniture finishing and leather upholstery was done. This space would later become the "modeled" leather department.

This photograph of the furniture/bindery in 1909 was taken from Walnut Street (the back yard of Alex Fournier), looking east.

The last major building of the Roycroft Campus was the power house, built in 1909–1910 of rusticated concrete block. The so-called fireproof building housed coal-fired steam generators, which provided electricity and heat to the Roycroft buildings in an underground system. As with most power plants of its day, the machinery at Roycroft operated on "DC" current. The second floor housed a large room used for practice by the Roycroft bands. After the Roycroft Shops closed, this building became the second of the campus structures to become a church. In 1970, an attorney converted it into medical and law offices and apartments. In February 1997, the building was almost destroyed by a fire. Plans are under way for its eventual restoration.

Constructed of local stone, half-timbered and stuccoed in the style of a small English cottage, the second blacksmith shop initially had a brick interior and a dirt floor. The blacksmiths created hardware for doors, furniture, lighting fixtures, andirons, and tools for all the buildings on the Roycroft Campus. Mastersmith Peter Robarge (pictured to the left in the doorway) had been employed at Roycroft since 1899. The building was completed in 1902 at the end of the Appian Way, directly across from the Roycroft Inn, which would open in 1903.

At the end of the Roycroft's Appian Way is the quaint and charming stone building with a tile roof that was the blacksmith shop, and later, the copper shop. The walkway between the Roycroft Inn and the Roycroft Shops connected both sides of South Grove Street on the Roycroft Campus. It is presently under reconstruction and restoration. The sale of bricks inscribed with supporters' names and dates will raise the needed restoration funds. As with other renovated Roycroft buildings, it will be better than ever. The RALA is following through, "Not as Hubbard did it back then, but as he would do it now."

Organized in 1904 under the private banking laws of New York State, the Roycroft had its own bank called "Elbert Hubbard Banker." Bert Hubbard was promoted to head cashier in charge at the time this brochure photograph was taken. A large wing (unseen) was added at the rear to house the Roycroft Copper Shop.

By 1923, the approximate time of this postcard, the Roycroft Copper Shop had grown from the small blacksmith shop to the Art Metal department headed by ex-banker "Fra Baldini" (Karl Kipp), who is shown here with toddler Elbert Hubbard III (known as John) feeding the tame white doves.

Through the early 1900s and into the 1920s, Roycroft's hammered-copper items were in great demand. Two additions, one housing production and the other for the finishing room (right), were completed c. 1918. This latter room was used to bottle East Aurora maple syrup and honey in the 1930s and 1940s under the Roycroft Shops and later Roycroft Products Labels.

Taken c. 1958, this shop is now called the Roycroft Gift Shop. Since it was the last shop to be producing when the Roycrofters went out of business in 1938, the trademark name "Roycroft" and the famous orb mark were sold with this building. It operated as a showroom through the 1940s and 1950s for many of the Roycroft craftsmen who continued living and working in East Aurora. The original Karl Kipp (Too-Kay Shop) stained-glass and leaded-glass lanterns hang on either side of the entrance.

This boulder was dragged up from the creek and installed in July 1916 with a grand celebration on the lawn in front of the print shop, facing Main Street. It was a tribute to Alive and Elbert Hubbard.

A bronze plaque heralds the memory of Elbert and Alice Hubbard on this famous boulder. It was Elbert and Alice's only memorial; their bodies were never recovered from the Irish Sea.

Three
THE ROYCROFT INN

No one knows who coined the term for the Roycroft Inn, "The Jewel in the crown of the Roycroft Campus." The magic of the place is two-fold; its unplanned growth and unfolding space create what philosopher and art critic John Ruskin (1819–1901) referred to as the "spirit of artisans and the purity of necessity." The room at the top of the Roycroft Inn is the Ruskin Room, under it is the Morris Room, and on the main floor, the room that was Hubbard's own library is over the first Roycroft Presses, which were in the cellars.

Exhilaration is felt at the Roycroft Inn because of the location. The site is said to have originally been Native-American holy ground. In 1984, it was doused as a power point containing enlivened energy of a magnetic nature.

The Roycroft Inn was very different in appearance in its final form (1905) than the medieval-looking buildings across South Grove Street that make up the Roycroft Chapel and Shops. The finished Roycroft Inn is perceived as a prairie-style building, not unlike those of Frank Lloyd Wright. The south end is Chicago style, with curtain wall construction. Much has been made of its similarity to Wright's efforts for Darwin Martin and the Larkin Company in Buffalo at the same time (1903–1905). Hubbard and Martin were close friends; Hubbard was Martin's mentor, in fact. Of course, the Roycrofters were ready to duplicate the architect's genius in wood. Our photographs and drawings trace the construction and evolution of the structure that did, indeed, seem to grow like topsy. There is no architect on record, and the oral history regarding blueprints is a fine story told by Anthony Rohr. He claims that, as a young man, when his father ran the inn in the late 1930s, he found in the cellar of the Roycroft Inn a set of plans on linen material. He used them to patch his bi-plane.

The small, church-like building with Gothic-style windows and cupola (built in 1897) was enlarged with a two-story addition in 1899 and a large south wing in 1900. The footprint grew to encompass Hubbard's own home by 1903. He tore down his Victorian house and laid the Roycroft Inn on the foundation. The rooms of the inn behind that portion were constructed soon after. A plaque in the Roycroft Inn Music Salon (now the lobby) documents that "Alice Hubbard–Designer, Alex Fournier–Painter and James Cadzow–Architect (wood worker)" redesigned that room in 1905. The entire building has been beautifully restored. The Roycroft Inn reopened for the 100th anniversary of the founding of the Roycroft Press. A gigantic gift to the Arts & Crafts Revival by the Margaret L. Wendt Foundation, $8 million and eight years, went into the effort. Today, the Roycroft Inn has 22 suites and features dining rooms that seat 200. It is once again one of the most beautiful buildings and interiors in the Arts & Crafts style.

The first print shop, completed in February 1998, would become the reception room of the Roycroft Inn in 1903. Anson Blackman, known to Roycrofters as "Ali Baba," stands in front of the Gothic-style country building that Hubbard claimed to be based on St. Oswald's Church (where Wordworth is buried in the churchyard in Grasmere, England). Blackman was a key figure in Roycroft lore. With him are two small girls, one of whom is possibly Elbert and Bertha's only daughter, Katherine (1896–1961).

The interior of the original print shop (1898) became the Roycroft Inn reception room in 1903. (Note the fireplace to the far right. It appears often in subsequent photographs.) The clubhouse atmosphere of this gaslit interior was captured by the famous documentary photographer Frances Benjamin Johnson. A faint pencil signature appears in the right corner. The round table in the foreground, with the octagonal legs and cannonball feet, marks the first appearance of the Roycroft furniture that was soon to be offered for sale. Two examples of this form are extant in East Aurora today.

Ali Baba, posed with an early lawnmower, stands just north of Elbert and Bertha's home on South Grove Street. Visible in the foreground is the print shop (c. 1900), with its third addition to the right. The shop later became the Roycroft Inn reception room and main dining room.

Looking across muddy South Grove Street is the Roycroft Phalanstery. This photo was taken in the summer, near the turn of the century. Notice the porch on the house (left), which in later years would be discarded when the building was incorporated into the expanding Roycroft Inn. To the rear of the drive is a two-story wooden building that housed the Roycroft staff. A cupola atop the second addition of the Roycroft Inn completes the Gothic-windowed impression of a country church. Beneath that is the John Ruskin Room, which is over the William Morris Room. Under this room, on the first floor, is the room that housed Elbert Hubbard's library, which was available for the workers. Below the library, the Roycroft Presses printed Arts & Crafts philosophy to send worldwide.

Looking northeast from the Hubbard home's walk, we can see the original Roycroft building with its two additions. The chimney is decorative, and the windows are both Gothic-style and plain. At this point in time, the Roycroft Printing Shop already employed more than four dozen people. The workers were producing *The Philistine* magazine and a monthly publication called *Little Journeys*. The business was growing very rapidly due to the success of the March 1899 "Message to Garcia."

In a view from the balcony of the second-floor Morris Room, looking down into the collating room of the south wing, this rare photograph shows the space as a work room. Another addition was soon added, and this room became the Roycrofters' dining hall.

The the third-floor Ruskin Room, under the cupola, reveals a pyramidal vaulted ceiling and walls of pine beadboard. The dapper young artist in the picture is Samuel Warner, the Roycroft art director at the time. The young women and men under his tutelage are illuminating the fine Roycroft Press books by hand. Notice the gas lighting in this early picture.

Most of the illuminators at this time came to work in their Sunday best, as seen in this photograph of the Morris Room. The large fireplace, radiators, and large windows provided pleasant working conditions.

Located on the main floor of the Phalanstery, the east room addition was called the Oak Room until c. 1903, when it became the library. The bulk of the library's collection was from Hubbard's personal library. Of note is the early, round oak table with octagonal legs and cannonball feet. A few of these still exist today. A terra-cotta bust of Elbert Hubbard by Jerome Connor is displayed here.

The first floor of the original building had, by 1900, become an all-purpose room for taking orders, shipping, and mailing. It was lit by gas and heated by a beautiful brick fireplace, which has an arched opening and a pair of seahorse andirons designed by Denslow and executed by Connor. A replica, *Winged Victory of Samothrace*, graces a shelf on the left—*Shades of Frank Lloyd Wright*.

Here we see the famous Roycroft Peristyle, or connecting porch system, under construction. The photo was taken just outside the front door and shows a group of about two dozen Roycroft carpenters directed by foreman William Roth (seated to the left in a white shirt, jacket, and tie). The porch was to connect the first building with the hotel rooms to the south.

This postcard view, looking south at the finished Roycroft Inn Peristyle, is an excellent perspective of the stone wall. The young man on the steps is Dard Hunter, the recently arrived artist who soon became the next Roycroft art director. The sign says "Why not use the sidewalk."

A canopy of elm trees graced both sides of South Grove Street when this c. 1909 photograph was taken of a serene and complete Roycroft Inn.

A simple fountain with native plantings is central to the courtyard formed by the dining room and the wooden porch system. The space was a favorite for both Roycroft workers and guests.

This photograph looks in the opposite direction from south to north at the newly finished Roycroft Inn c. 1905. The building, with its wrap-around Prairie Peristyle design, is a complete change from the medieval stone buildings that were built across the street to house the Roycroft Shops. Impressive and grand, the peristyle clearly resembles the pergola at the Darwin Martin House that was designed by Frank Lloyd Wright in nearby Buffalo. The two were built around the same time.

This photograph, taken by Charles Kingsbury and dated 1910, shows the summer garden fully developed. The statue of Michelangelo by Paul Bartlett across the street is visible between the pines decorating the peristyle. According to Nancy Hubbard Brady, Elbert and Bertha's granddaughter, these small evergreens were a gift from J.D. Rockefeller. Look carefully at the recently installed stained-glass and clear-leaded tulip glass windows designed and made by Dard Hunter.

About 1912, Elbert and Alice commissioned her friend and fellow feminist Katherine Maltwood to design a sculpture for the south lawn of the Roycroft Inn. Named *Magna Mater*, it is a tribute to the travail of women. This photo clearly shows the curtain wall construction of the facade, which was done in the Chicago style.

Buffalo snow on the Roycroft south lawn almost obscures *Magna Mater*. The teahouse Twill Do is in the background, on the right side of the inn.

A 1913 postcard with mature wisteria leads us to believe that the Roycroft Teahouse is already several years old. Between lunch and dinner, a cup of tea "Twill do" gave the small building behind the inn its name. Lemonade, ice cream, and cookies were also served here. Elbert and Alice's daughter Miriam had her first job here working as a hostess and server.

Mrs. Robert Charles from Canada is shown here in September 1914 while on her honeymoon at Roycroft, enjoying the peristyle that was furnished in Old Hickory.

The Roycroft furniture in this rare photo appears to have been just delivered and assembled. The first print shop was about to become the Roycroft Inn reception room. The early furniture shown here (c. 1902) is highly collectible today. We're looking at the front door; the fireplace is just out of sight on the left.

In another view of the print shop, this 1909 postcard shows the interior of the reception room, with the stairs on the right, the wall treatment of burlap with leather straps and tacking, Navajo rugs, and Dard Hunter lanterns with heart cut-outs.

Looking from the front doorway in the opposite direction, you are now facing the stairs that lead up to the Morris and Ruskin Rooms. A rare, Roycroft grandfather clock is seen on the middle back wall. Two Morris chairs with tufted horse hair are also pictured. There is a beveled mirror above the mantle and two Ali Baba benches on either side of the fireplace.

Between 1910 and 1930, the reception room was redecorated. The high-backed benches on either side of the fireplace could be moved into a perpendicular position to form an inglenook that protected visitors from winter winds. Businessmen read in double Morris chairs by the fireside. The Gothic-style windows are decorated with Dard Hunter's stained-glass, stylized tulips. The dormer windows, which remain clear glass to this day, are once again visible after the false ceiling was removed in the 1995 restoration.

Opening off of the reception room, on the left, is the door to Alice Hubbard's office. The unique, Dard Hunter pottery lamp with the stained-glass shade is still in the Hubbard family. Jerome Connor's sculpture of mother and child is seen on her desk, and to the right of the door is his bas relief of William Morris. You can clearly see the burlap wall treatment and Native-American rugs here. What you cannot see is the carved, leather frieze in the office that depicted the seasons of the year—roses for spring, cherries for summer, grapes for autumn, and pine cones for winter. The handsome, beamed ceiling is not shown here, but it has been nicely restored in the present-day Roycroft Inn ladies' room.

The John Ruskin Room on the third floor became one of two VIP suites when the early print shop building was converted into the Roycroft Inn. Private baths were added to Ruskin and Morris Rooms, and guests enjoyed the existing fireplaces in each room. All the furniture and lighting was made in the Roycroft Furniture and Copper Shops. The Dard Hunter lantern with heart cut-outs illuminates the rare trestle table that has "Roycroft" carved on the side. According to an early promotional booklet, the curtains were made of green velvet and the burlap walls were medium green. The floors were made of maple and the pine-bead board vaulted ceiling is spectacular. This room no longer has public access.

Dard Hunter's hanging chandeliers with heart cut-outs in a triangular form with frosted shades (c. 1905) replaced early gaslights. They were used in the large, main dining room. A plate rail and window ledges display pottery, probably Teco, although Roycroft made pottery for two or three years. This was after 1903, when Alexis Jean Fournier came to Roycroft to work as director of the Roycroft Art Gallery. His 1902 masterpiece, *Entrance to the Grand Canal in Venice*, hangs at the south end of the room. Note the hanging inspirational signs made of rough slabs of wood that read "Good Cheer," "Reciprocity," and "Fletcherize." Horace Fletcher was a nutritionist who frequented Roycroft and admonished that you chew your food a hundred times. Most of the early Ali Baba benches have now been replaced by the first Roycroft dining room chairs.

Only a few years later, c. 1910, the main dining hall was been revised again with the new Vienna Secession-style lanterns, also by Dard Hunter. The lantern designs reflect his trip and studies abroad. A new style chair with vertical slats is also shown. Many of these pieces are still in use in this room today. Fournier's painting of Venice would hang here until 1987. Today, it is the property of the authors and rests atop the mantle in the original copper shop. Plans are afoot to get it into the possession of a major museum.

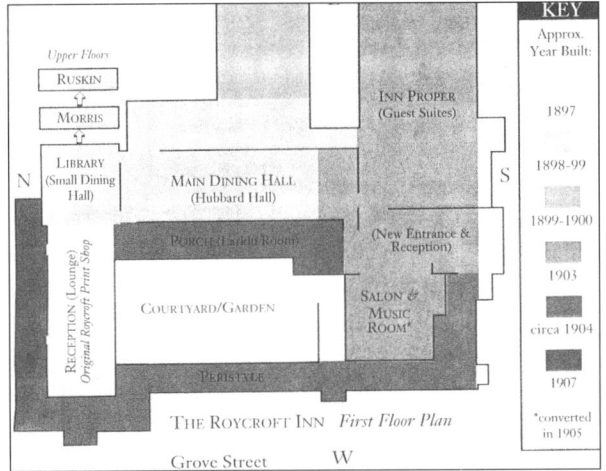

This drawing of the footprint of the Roycroft Inn recently appeared in *The Roycroft Inn*, a book edited by Jennifer Lewis. The plan was provided by author Robert Rust, but it is not his; Elbert (Bert) Hubbard II passed it on to his biographer, Charles Hamilton. It shows how the building grew like topsy as need demanded, creating one of the most handsome Arts & Crafts commercial interiors in the United States. As its former innkeepers, we can attest to the inconvenience it places on the staff and the special magnetism it holds for visitors.

Bird's eye or tiger maple furniture and wood trim graced the Elizabeth Barrett Room and three other suites at the Roycroft Inn. Most accommodations were arranged with an interior dressing room and sitting room lit by sheer-curtained windows that let in natural light and looked into the individual unheated sleeping porch. The fresh-air out-of-doors practice was part of the Arts & Crafts philosophy and architecture not only at Roycroft, but in bungalows everywhere. Each room had a guest book in which the occupants kept up a running dialogue. The four maple Morris chairs were found in the Emerson, Disraeli, Wagner, and Barrett Rooms, and all are recorded today. One is on loan to the Hubbard/Roycroft Museum, one is in Hollywood, another is at the Metropolitan Museum of Art in New York City, and the last is at the Fournier House.

The Roycroft Inn booklet, published c. 1908, promoted all the rooms of note in the hotel. The library housed Elbert Hubbard's private collection of European and American metaphysical, history, and art books and magazines, which were available to guests and workers alike. This image, entitled "A Corner in the Library," indicates the elegance of the rustic setting. An Ali Baba bench is shown in the foreground beside the stone fireplace, and the quartersawn oak bench with library shelves (behind the library table) is one of a pair. Both are in service in the Morris Room at the Roycroft Inn today.

A view of the opposite corner of the library reveals bookcases, study areas, and more artwork, most of it by Roycroft artists Alex Fournier, Sandor Landeau, Eleanor Douglas, and Carl Ahrens. A quote in the late Roycroft Inn promotion booklet reads as follows: "Pure literature and good books are meat and drink. They are the silos that feed the mind, nourishing and energizing it." Today, this room is the lovely library dining room.

"This is a booklet of facts about Elbert Hubbard's Roycroft Inn" reads an even later advertising piece. By this time, the corners of the peristyle have been incorporated into additional public rooms. This is the south corner known as "the Sun Parlor and Lounge," or writing room. The caption indicates it is a place to chat and, on cool evenings, a corner for tête-à-têtes.

Created by designer Alice Hubbard, architect James Cadzow, and artist Alex Fournier, the Roycroft Music Salon is possibly the most beautiful Arts & Crafts room anywhere in the nation. "America" is the name of the Roycroft mural that is part of the frieze decorating this special space. Known to many as the "eight man-made wonders of the world," the murals are fascinating and beautiful works of art painted by Fournier in his Walnut Street studio. A parade of Roycrofters carried them to the inn in 1905 and lifted them into place. Ninety years later, the murals have been fully restored by the Conservation School at Buffalo State College; the historic day the murals were brought to the inn was recreated as a true victory celebration. Monies for the over $100,000 project were donated by the Roycroft Revitalization Corporation (RRC). The alcove to the right housed the Steinway Grand Piano and another set of murals entitled "Times of the Day." They depict scenes from sunrise to moonrise and are similar to the companion series in the Fournier House.

To the left of the salon, in the northeast corner, is the entry to the south end of the building and the salon. The murals that created this foyer, including two studies and Fournier's "Seasons of the Year," have been lost. We know there was a mural of late winter, and of "early spring maple "sugaring, which is still a serious occupation in East Aurora. The most prominent mural of Venice in the main room, showing the Church of Santa Maria Majorie, received the most serious conservation and restoration; it was completed in August 1996, more than a year after the inn reopened. The half walls with doric columns on either side are pure Arts & Crafts design. The important chair was one of two used by Hubbard and his guest lecturers for Sunday night talks. One is at the Hubbard/Roycroft Museum and the other is still in the Hubbard family.

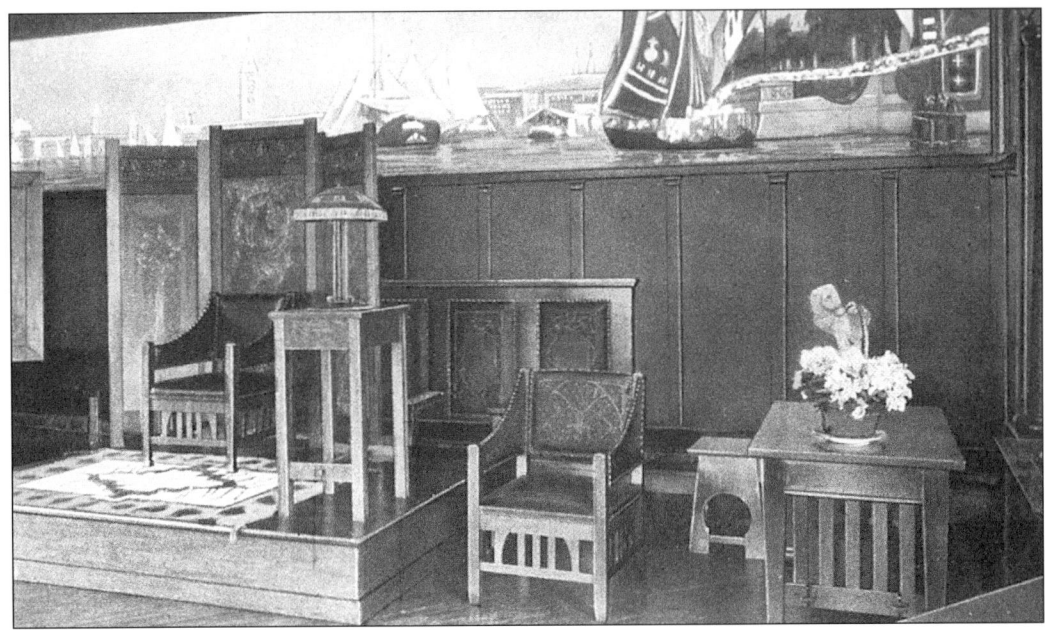

Shown here are the lecture platform and two English-style, carved leather Roycroft chairs. The screen was also made of embossed and gilded leather. The one-of-a-kind lamp and the screen are part of a private collection that remains in East Aurora; both have been loaned to various exhibitions.

It was once called the "Outdoor Dining Room" but was enclosed c. 1907 and has been called the Larkin Room since 1971. Overlooking the courtyard, it was used mostly in fair weather. The table lamps and ceiling lights are probably Dard Hunter designs. Five pair of french doors connected to the main dining room, and a screen door to the outdoor court made this space versatile as well as light and airy; it was a popular breakfast room. It still seats 50 people and remains the place where breakfast is served.

This September 1914 view looks southeast at the 1909 final peristyle design that connected the c. 1880 house to the north of the Roycroft Inn to the hotel proper. With the new porch in place, special guests could walk under cover to the dining room. This building would house Thomas Edison and his entourage as well as Henry Ford and his large family. In the 1930s, it became the manager's quarters, and in 1940, it served as the home of Samuel Guard, the new owner of the Roycroft Campus, following the Roycrofters' bankruptcy. The connection was destroyed in the 1950s to large trucks room for deliveries. It is planned that this building will be restored to guest rooms complete with peristyle connection.

One of the best views of the completed peristyle, this photograph was taken in the winter of 1940 by well-known photographer Allen Sipprell. The tree-lined Appian Way to the right is the special walkway connecting the two sides of the street.

Shown here is a front and center view of the main entrance to the Roycroft Inn. This image shows the newly laid brick foundation to the peristyle c. 1920. Notice that the cupola is gone; it was removed in 1910.

The beautiful reception room became a bar room in 1940. The ceiling was lowered, the grand stairway was removed, and only the fireplace and a few chairs remain. Note the jukebox where the grandfather clock used to stand.

Edwin Miller bought the Roycroft Inn in 1950 and was determined to bring the place back to life. An avid supporter of the Buffalo Bills football team, he persuaded them to use the inn as a summer training camp for five years. Decorative pieces typical of the day, webbed aluminum porch chairs, a "modern" telephone booth, and a neon sign gave the building an updated flair. Restoration was not yet a gleam in anyone's eye.

By the 1960s, the Roycroft Inn was the town's central gathering place, unlike the mecca for new thought and national visitors that it had been in the early 1900s. Rotary and other service clubs thought of it as community property. All the major events of a lifetime were held here, from dancing school to engagement and wedding celebrations, anniversary parties, retirement dinners, and funeral breakfasts.

Most of the Roycroft Inn's owners, including Bert Hubbard, endured bankruptcy. One or two prospered as the Roycroft Inn continued to be a central community force. In 1964, the worst financial disaster saw most of the furnishings and artwork sold at auction.

In 1971, the Turgeon family bought the Roycroft Inn. With the direction and inspiration given to author Kitty Turgeon by Nancy Hubbard Brady, red-flocked wallpaper was removed, as well as sculptured carpet, mod curtains, wagon-wheel lighting fixtures, white woodwork, and a piano bar. Purchasing the original Roycroft furniture back from the community was not difficult; it was worth very little. Some of the furniture was donated. This was the beginning of the Roycroft Renaissance.

Four
ROYCROFT ARTISANS AND WORKERS

Perhaps no other utopian craft community embraced as wide a range of artistic endeavors as did the Roycrofters. Although the main intent and actual sales reflected the devotion to the printing enterprise, this paternalistic community founded and led by Elbert Hubbard produced a stunning variety of beautiful objects and art works. The skills of those involved developed in an apprentice system and were equally diverse. From the trained artisans like Alex Fournier and Louis Kinder to the talented Dard Hunter and Karl Kipp, who developed their creative skills at Roycroft and passed them on to the boys and girls "right off the farm." The approximately 500 people who participated in Roycroft were devoted, diverse, and decidedly Roycrofters. They worked together, played together, and married one another; in their synergetic efforts, they found joy but not a great deal of money. A fair number stayed for a year or so, a few came and went, and some stayed for life.

Several generations of descendants have produced artists, scholars, musicians, and just plain folks to add to East Aurora's Roycroft stock. Many of the original artisans and workers went on to fame elsewhere—Dard Hunter became a leading authority on paper making; W.W. Denslow illustrated the *Wizard of Oz* for L. Frank Baum; Wally Schang became a major league ball player; and Jerome Connor left to head up the metal arts department for Gustav Stickley's Craftsman Company. He eventually returned to Ireland, where he was—and still is—regarded as a major sculptor and National Treasure. Alex Fournier, along with Karl Kipp, George Scheide Mantel, and Walter Jennings, remained at Roycroft until the end. They founded or went to work for other companies in western New York or retired and enjoyed life in East Aurora after the Roycrofters went out of business in 1938.

Several of the distinguished artisans belonged to the Boston Society of Arts & Crafts and often freelanced on their own. Our conversations years ago with Miriam Hubbard Roelofs, Nancy Hubbard Brady, Emil Sahlin, George and Gladys ScheideMantel, Rix Jennings, and so many others historically involved and all now deceased, gave us the impression that Elbert Hubbard was their hero; he was totally in charge.

In 1899, the Roycroft Chapel was completed and housed the Roycroft Library. This was prior to Alex Fournier's arrival, when the art gallery became the main attraction. This photograph of the one-story, wood building is rare. It is the only known photograph of the exterior of the first blacksmith shop, where local smiths perfected the craft of making iron hardware and andirons under the aegis of the Roycroft name. It was also Jerome Connor's first studio and the home of the short-lived (from 1899 to 1901) Roycroft Pottery. The stones for the Roycroft Print Shop are in the foreground. South Grove Street was still a dirt road with a plank sidewalk at the time. The Roycroft's stone walls had yet to be built.

Newell White of the firm White & Wagonner is pictured here working for the Roycrofters c. 1899. His press, the Pendennis Press, was purchased by Hubbard and moved to the new building on the campus in early 1897.

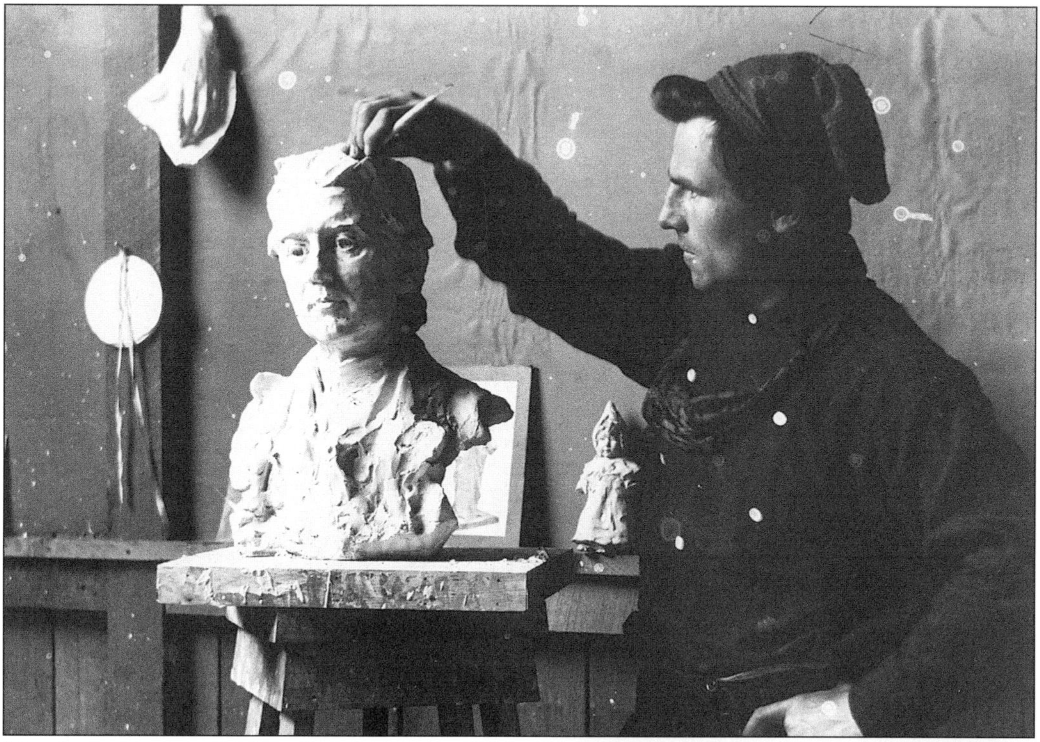

"St. Gerome" Connor (1874–1943) is shown here in the first blacksmith shop, which also served as his studio. He was born in Annascul, County Kerry, a small village on the Dingle Peninsula in Ireland. When he was a boy, Connor came to the United States with his family to settle in Salem, Massachusetts. There he met Samuel Warner, and in 1898, at the urging of a friend of Elbert Hubbard's, they came to Roycroft. Once here, he was instrumental in helping build the buildings and in designing books and metalwork. We believe it was Jerome Connor, known foremost for his sculpture, who designed and sculpted the bas relief of the "north wind" on the face of the Roycroft Chapel. In 1899, the Roycrofters issued a catalog of "the sculpture of St. Gerome." Connor met and married his wife at Roycroft before leaving to join Stickley in July 1902.

This photograph from the 1900 *Book of the Roycrofters* is entitled "A Roycroft Artist." We believe it is a young Bert Hubbard. He is breaking stones for the print shop. In the medieval tradition of designing while building, every worker was an artist and was expected to "pitch in" for every task.

"Old Uncle John—Woodworker and Horse Trainer" is also from the *Book of the Roycrofters*. This portrait was reproduced as one of the first Roycroft postcards in 1899. John was a study for one of Connor's busts.

Lyle Hawthorne, "The Red One," poses for the book c. 1900, in front of the door that could have been at Elbert's own house. We believe it is now the door of the Fournier House.

Many young women learned the art of book binding at Roycroft in the guild system of training on the job. Here they are working on sewing frames and stitching books in the first print shop. The print shop staff was expanding rapidly after the success of the essay "The Message to Garcia."

The second Roycroft Blacksmith Shop was built in 1902 from the stones left over from the construction of the chapel and the print shop. In the picture are the same workers as in the first photo with Peter Robarge, master smith, in the doorway (p. 41). His wife also worked at Roycroft as an illuminator. Here, in this quaint structure that was made to resemble an English cottage with a tile roof, they made the unsigned andirons that not only furnished the Roycroft fireplaces, but also were for sale in the first *Somethings for Sale at the Roycroft Shops* catalogue.

A very young Rixford Jennings (1906–1996) poses on the side steps of the big print shop in front of his father, Walter Jennings, who had come from Troy, New York, to learn the art of book binding. At the time of this picture, Walter was an apprentice, along with Karl Kipp, to start the Roycroft Art Metal Shop in the expanding blacksmith shop.

Carl Ahrens (1862-1936) was one of many Canadians drawn across the border to Roycroft. He and his cousin, Eleanor Douglas, started the short-lived Roycroft Pottery. They were both potters and fine artists who were well known for painting trees. Ahrens was an instructor at the Arts & Crafts school at Chautauqua in 1898 when we believe he first met Hubbard, who invited him to Roycroft.

In the last row of this image (center) is Elbert Hubbard and Lt. Col. Andrew Rowan, who was made famous by "The Message to Garcia," first published as a untitled essay in the March 1899 issue of *The Philistine*. Also included in this photograph of Roycroft employees and department heads are the following: (far right, last row) Alex Fournier, director of the Roycroft Art Gallery; editor George Wharton James; (seated on the bottom three steps, from second left to right) Elbert's sons, Sandy, Bert, and Ralph Hubbard.

Captain Rowan's unswerving devotion to performing the delivery of a packet to the Cuban General Garcia in the Spanish-American War inspired Hubbard to write the homily or preachment on following through without excuses or deviation. It became the fifth most printed piece of literature after the Bible, and remains in print today. The Dale Carnegie Course uses it, and it is given to every Air Force Cadet. This is the first booklet, reissued on the 1897 letter press by the new Roycroft Print Shop & Museums.

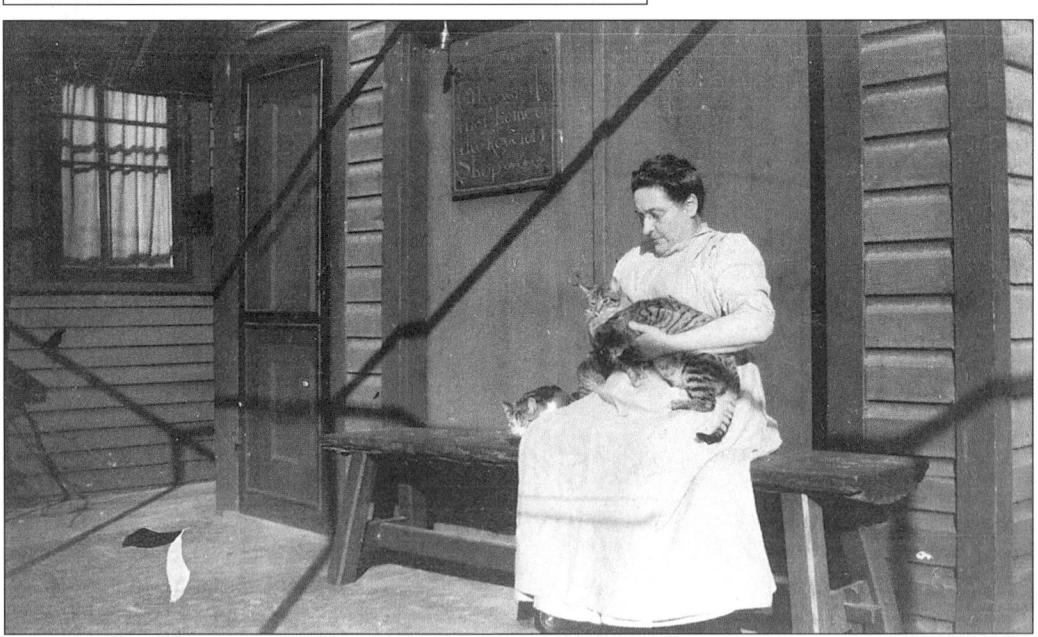

Known as "Mother Grant," Ellen Dearden Grant (1861–1946) served as one of the first Roycroft chefs. She is shown here outside the inn's kitchen door talking with her cat "Moley," resting on an extremely long Ali Baba bench (c. 1910). Of course, she washed her hands before returning to her cooking!

The Roycroft Shop
in East Aurora
Erie County
New York

Ali Baba and June

We don't know the names of all the workers but we do recognize the animals! This postcard is titled "Ali Baba & June." The valet, handyman, and horse trainer was a Hubbard family friend and often served as Elbert's alter ego when Hubbard wanted to say something that he didn't want attributed to him, such as "art is largely a matter of haircut" or "two in the bush is the root of all evil." His real name was Anson Blackman. He was born in nearby Marilla, New York.

The Roycroft farm was the subject of another postcard titled "The Threshers," c. 1909. We see only Hubbard's back, but Alice is clearly visible with papers in hand. The 36 workers shown here indicate that besides a growing farm crew, other employees literally "pitched in" for haying and threshing. The Roycrofters had four farms providing sustenance to the operation. Chickens, Guinea hens, cows, pigs, and maple syrup in woodlots were just outside of town.

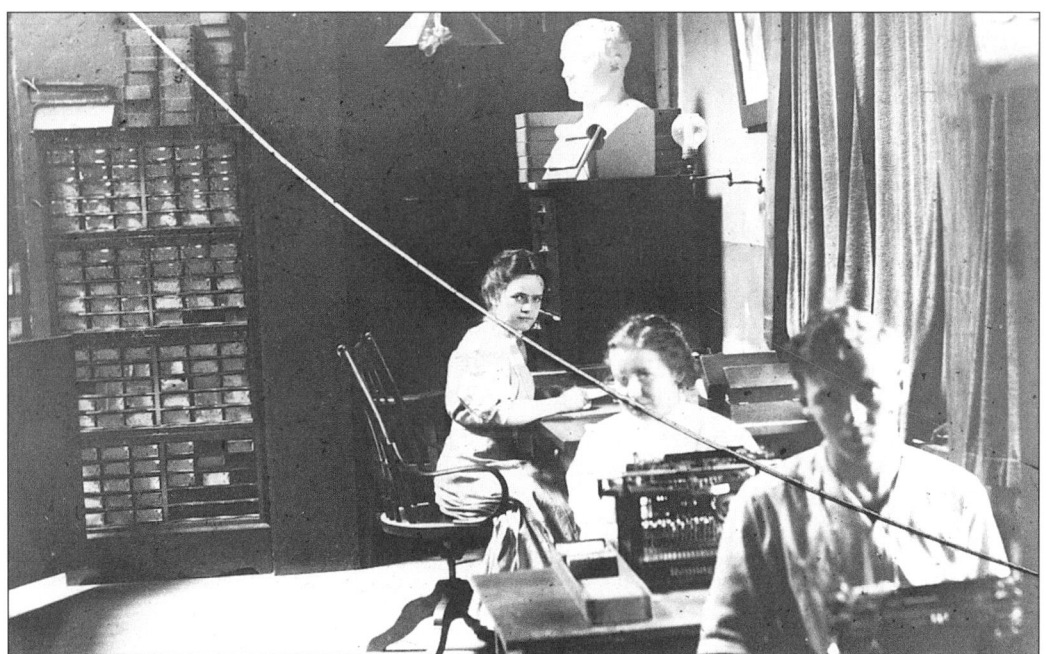

Working conditions in turn-of-the-century industrial sites were horrendous. A goal of the Roycroft was to provide the best possible staff environment. This ideal was a principle tenet of the Arts & Crafts philosophy that was practiced at Roycroft with steadfast honesty and above and beyond the call. Secretarial work had been a man's job; Roycroft was first to give over that work to women. Shown here, two girls and one fellow are hard at work in the new print shop. Notice the gas lights. The photograph dates prior to 1909.

With the advent of electricity and the completion of the Roycroft Power House, all of the modern printing equipment was available. These two workers are using a mechanized folding machine for wrapping the *The Philistine* magazine, which had 225,000 subscribers after 1910.

On the second floor, above the presses, are mostly women workers, professionally dressed in starched white blouses and ready to assemble the mailings of the just completed *Philistine*. All the cabinets to the left were made at the Roycroft Furniture Shop.

Sammy the Artist was the name given to Samuel Warner, the Roycroft's first art director. He came to Roycroft along with Jerome Conner in 1898 and left to return to Massachusetts to teach in 1904.

After the death of founder Elbert Hubbard and his second wife, Alice, the department heads were assembled and photographed for the September 1915 *Fra* magazine. The Roycroft Chapel is in the background. Pictured are Herbert Buffin (furniture), Ernest Simmons (secretary), Fritz

Kranz (leather), Cy Rosen (printing), Felix Shay (printing), Karl Kipp (copper), Bert (now in charge), and Sandy Hubbard (grounds superintendent).

Rix Jennings said the din of the copper shop was what gave it the name "Anvil Chorus." On the far left of this 1916 photo is Fra Baldini (Karl Kipp), head of the copper shop, looking unhappy to be assembled for a picture. Twenty-five or more have ceased work to pose. Later, women worked in the copper shop as finishers and platers. By 1916, Bert had convinced Kipp to return and expand the shop. Art Cole (wearing an apron) is second from right in the front row and Walter Jennings is behind him to the left.

This modified, four-square house was built for a Roycroft employee on West Fillmore Street in East Aurora about four blocks northeast of the campus. It stands today unmodified. It is made of state-of-the-art concrete block, a fireproof construction material.

A block and a half north of the Roycroft Inn, almost across the street from Bert's log cabin, stood this large, turn-of-the-century building. To the right of the house are cornfields. Farmland was only three blocks north of the Roycroft Campus. This c. 1907 photograph was taken by Paul Fournier, a Roycroft employee and noted photographer who exhibited worldwide. He was Alex Fournier's son, and his studio was located on Main Street.

Everything on the Roycroft Campus was not all work and no play! On the second and top floor of the power house (built c. 1909), space was available for practicing theatricals, band practice, and club meetings. These 18 all-male employees seem to enjoy posing for the photographer. Notice the electric lights, Roycroft chairs, and especially, the new-fangled sprinkler system. Unfortunately in February 1997 a fire destroyed much of the building. It is being rebuilt.

Music was a large part of the Roycroft community, and this 16-piece cornet band gave Roycroft workers yet another opportunity for recreation. The young clarinet player kneeling in the lower right of the first row is shown at left on the porch of his East Aurora home in his uniform, which was supplied by the Roycrofters.

This Roycroft Concert Band had 23 members. There was also a marching band and a German Band. The two-story power house and the three-story furniture shop are in the background. This c. 1915 image indicates the variety of music available to the Roycrofters. The drum is in the Hubbard/Roycroft Museum.

The Roycroft baseball team had a high profile on the campus. The semi-professional team played all over the United States. Exhibitions of this type were common in early-20th-century baseball. Three players from the Roycroft team became professionals; the most famous was Wally Schang of the Cleveland Indians, who played and managed teams until the early 1950s. Team members pictured are, from left to right, as follows: (front row) Al Miller, Clarence White, Jack Tarnish, Bob Schang, and Billy Schumaker; (middle row) Theodore Fleming, Charlie Wright (manager), and Arthur Garret; (back row) Herb Bowen, Francis Bowen, Chris Shopper, Ralph Wheeler, Roy Wheeler, and Allen Bowen.

Baseball was also a recreation for other workers and guests and was played in Hamlin Park on some summer afternoons, mostly weekends. Games were a highlight of the Roycroft conventions.

OH, No—not exactly a HOE-DOWN, but just a plain, old-fashioned dance, where we all can mix things up a bit and the oldest among us be the youngest. It will be at the Roycroft Ballroom on FRIDAY EVENING, FEB. 12— Lincoln's Birthday—under the management of the Roycroft Base Ball Club. Ample refreshments—both hot and cold —will be served to those who must have them, at a slight extra charge.

The music will consist of a three-piece orchestra, who will see to it that music for plenty of square dances will be played, so Deacon Buffum won't need to be a wall-flower.

Tickets are Fifty Cents each—admitting you and She—they can be had from any member of the ball team.

So, there now!

Fund-raisers were an activity of sports teams, even at the turn of the century. This c. 1903 flyer promotes the Lincoln's birthday hoedown.

During the summer of 1916, on the lawn of the west side of the Roycroft Campus, as many department heads and workers as possible were assembled for a corporate photograph. One hundred and forty-six are represented and at least twice that many weren't in the photo. Included here are Bert (Elbert Hubbard II) and Sandy Hubbard, Felix Shay, the Sahlin Brothers, Karl Kipp, Walter Jennings, and many others whose families have identified them over the last dozen years.

Elbert Hubbard poses by the well on the west lawn of the Roycroft Campus with a group of Roycroft workers. He referred to employees as the "Roycroft boys and girls," as many of them were young and right off the farm. There were also a number of more mature staff members.

Five

Visitors to the Campus and What They Saw

When the large bell on the corner of the print shop rang, it signaled a work break for the Roycrofters. Often, it was to gather on the lawn and meet a famous guest. Many of these guests would be on the platform for the Sunday night lecture or entertainment. Carrie Jacobs Bond, the composer and singer, might sing her famous "At the End of a Perfect Day." Clara Barton would discuss the Red Cross, which she founded. Actress Lillian Russel might recite a poem. Margaret Sanger could talk about the advantages of birth control, which she advocated nationwide. It is known that Susan B. Anthony was a visitor in her last years, as were many other feminists, or suffragettes, as they were called. We mention the well-known women first, not to downplay the many famous men who visited here, but to make it clear that both well-known men and women came to Roycroft.

Clarence Darrow, the lawyer well known for the Scopes Monkey Trial, and poet Carl Sandburg debated "Communism Versus Socialism" in the Roycroft Salon. Can you imagine the talk about town that stirred? J.D. Rockefeller, Henry Steinway, Harvey Firestone, and other business greats came and went. Thomas Edison, whose father-in-law founded nearby Chautauqua, was at Roycroft often. Harry Houdini was here in the the early 1900s, and even Frank Lloyd Wright travelled to Roycroft, although perhaps not until after the untimely death of Elbert and Alice Hubbard.

The list goes on and on, and I wish we had photographs of all of these people with a Roycroft building in the picture. Sadly, we do not, but we can show you many other guests and the buildings off the Roycroft Campus that they might have seen while they were here. The four Roycroft Farms and the Cazenovia Creek where they swam and canoed are pictured. Many visitors stayed at Emerson Hall, the Roycroft's secondary hotel; it is located on Prospect Street, two blocks from the Roycroft Inn. Bert Hubbard's log house, and later, his grand English Tudor manor house, were located about a mile from the Roycroft Campus. The center of the village, which was located on Main Street in East Aurora 100 years ago or less, is just blocks away. Several of the houses built for the artists and other master craftsmen are also nearby, as is Hamlin Park and the Roycroft Pavilion, the home of the Aurora Players for the past 65 years. The park is still a playground, ballpark, and music stage. Visitors still come from around the world making the pilgrimage to the most intact Arts & Crafts community still extant.

> # VISITORS
> at the Shop are always welcome, but the presence of the local agrarian—with time to incinerate—who comes here solely to visit the workers, is not desired ❧ Tell the lobscouse loafer we have work to do.

Shown here is one of the humorous and folksy mottos or epigrams Elbert Hubbard was known to write, print, and mail as well as post about the Roycroft Campus. You might say he created the sound bite.

George H. Daniels was one of the New York Central Railroad executives responsible for ordering millions of copies of "A Message to Garcia," thus bringing much fame and fortune to Roycroft.

George Wharton James, an English gentleman, was a Roycrofter at large; he was at Roycroft often but not in residence. Seen here on his Wonder Horse, he shared Hubbard's love of riding. James edited Roycroft books, was a collector and scholar of Native-American baskets, and wrote a biography on Joaquin Miller with Elbert Hubbard in 1903. He was an assistant editor of *The Craftsman* magazine for Gustav Stickley and was a founder of the Arroyo Culture in Pasadena at the turn of the 20th century. George Wharton James represents one of the leading figures in the Arts & Crafts movement, bringing English A&C attitudes and ideals to both coasts.

This c. 1903 postcard published by the Roycrofters bears the caption "Honest Roycrofters Three (more or less)." Marshall Wilder (center) is flanked by George Wharton James on the left and Hubbard on the right. Wilder was known as the pre-eminent humorist in the nation at this time. He was a frequent visitor at Roycroft, where a unique chair was designed for him to accommodate his special needs as a dwarf and a hunchback. The Marshall Wilder chair is rare and highly collectible. It has Mackmurdo feet and eventually was marketed and sold as a youth chair. Wilder was the editor of the ten-volume set *The Wit and Humor of America*.

Joaquin Miller (1837–1913) was known as the "poet of the Sierras" and was a dear friend of Elbert and Alice Hubbard. Miriam Hubbard Roelofs, their daughter, told the authors the story of how her father brought her to the hospital to see Miller on his death bed. Joaquin's real name was Cincinnatus Heine Miller. He lived in the hills of Oakland, California, where he had an "open-door policy" at his cabin when he was at home. Miller and the Hubbards visited back and forth on both sides of the United States. Elbert Hubbard wrote *A Little Journey to the Home of Joaquin Miller* in 1903.

B.J. Palmer, the founder of chiropractic medicine, is shown here with Elbert Hubbard at Palmer's home in Davenport, Iowa, on the Palmer College Campus. He and Elbert visited one another more than once. On his trips to East Aurora's Roycroft Campus, Palmer ordered Roycroft furniture, mottos, and books to furnish his institution. Many of these items are still on view at the school. Bert Hubbard (Elbert Hubbard II) wrote an essay entitled "Right Adjustment," an endorsement of chiropractic care. Ads for the curative powers of chiropractic procedures were in several Roycroft periodicals.

On the steps of the Roycroft Inn we see the Hubbard family, Roycroft staff, and distinguished visitors. A popular spot for posed pictures, this c. 1912 shot features Elbert's second family—his wife, Alice, and their young daughter Miriam (right). Also included is the mysterious Roycrofter-at-large, author and art critic Sadakichi Hartmann (back row, second from left) with goatee, mustache, and panama hat. The other guests and staff are not identified.

Again on the Roycroft Inn steps, Elbert poses with Freddie Welsh and airedale puppies, c. 1912. Welsh was an English boxer; in 1998 he was featured on the BBC when he was inducted into the Boxing Hall of Fame in Syracuse. Bert Hubbard always had airedales; we know one was named "Red." The breed was most popular from 1904 to 1922 and is considered to be the Arts & Crafts dog, especially during World War I. Our airedale, Mackmurdo, is the subject of a new artisan's alphabet, "A is for Airedale."

Unidentified but fascinating visitors appear in many of our records. Here, in a posed picture outside the print shop, Elbert and Alice are, as usual, the gracious host and hostess.

Author Eugene Grubb is shown in a typical pose on the Roycroft Inn's steps with Elbert and Alice on either side. The back of the photo notes that the little girl next to Alice is Lynnette, Elbert Hubbard II's eldest daughter, and that the young boys are "Roycroft School of Life" pupils. Also pictured are short-term secretary Mr. Grapek; Lorenzo Swartz, a master book binder; and Beulah Hood's brother, Stanley. Miss Hood was another one of the secretaries and a friend of Alice.

Across the lawn, on the west side of the Roycroft Campus looking toward Main Street, c. 1925, is the sculpture of Michelangelo by American artist Paul Bartlett. It was commissioned by Elbert Hubbard as a representation of great art for the Roycrofters. The gentleman posing with the statue in exactly the same stance as at the 1908 dedication of the piece, is the artist shortly before his death. Notice the memorial boulder (July 1916) in the background and the bronze turtle at the base of the plinth. Hubbard had complained about the lateness of the statue's delivery, and Bartlett attached the turtle with a note saying "Good art takes time."

Fifteen years after the sinking of the *Lusitania*, the monumental sculpture of Elbert Hubbard was unveiled on his birthday, June 19, 1930. Many distinguished guests were present. Shown from left to right are the following: the sculptor, Irishman Jerome Connor; editor and lecturer Joe Mitchell Chappel, a friend of Elbert's who had unveiled the memorial boulder 14 years before, at the 21st Annual Roycroft Convention; Chicago attorney Clarence Darrow; and Buffalo newspaper publisher Norman E. Mack, standing in conversation with Elbert Hubbard II.

Corporate executives (company unknown) are gathered for a formal picture during their annual meeting at the Roycroft Inn in the late 1920s or early 1930s. The Roycroft was a popular place for business conferences as well as for honeymooners and Arts and Crafts enthusiasts. Both Elbert and Bert were on excellent terms with corporate America.

A wide range of guests and entertainment was presented at the 23rd Annual Roycroft Convention. The long tradition of important speakers and varied activities continued through the twenties. An artist's talk by Roycroft court painter Alex Fournier and a hike led by master metalworker Karl Kipp were interspersed by lectures given by nutritionist Dr. H. Lindlar and Dr. Willard Carver, who was also a lawyer, discussing chiropractic care. Ball games, dancing, and weiner roasts, as well as hikes afield and a motor tour led by the Roycroft boys, were all part of the program.

This c. 1903 photograph, entitled "Hubbard and His Gang, Up the Creek," was probably taken at the Roycroft Camp on the shore of Cazenovia Creek, at what is now Emery Park. It was a favorite hike from the Roycroft for an overnight stay. Elbert is in the center and his son Ralph is to his right.

Three quarters of a mile down South Grove Street, there was a natural amphitheater and picnic ground used by the Roycrofters and guests. It was especially popular as a meeting place for the annual July Convention. This c. 1920 shot taken in the summer shows a guitar player (left) next to Bert (Elbert Hubbard II) and one of his daughters.

Shown in this view is Creekside Park, located on the south branch of Cazenovia Creek (later known as Donner's Grove). Roycroft visitors and locals rent canoes and motor about in the small steamboat *Winona*.

This photo postcard is entitled "Camp in the Roycroft Woods Where Little Journeys are Written, East Aurora, New York." This cabin was also famous as a horseback and hiking destination for guests and was known as the "Little Journeys Cabin." The postmark is 1906. After the turn of the century, it was here that most of the monthly *Little Journeys* were written by Elbert Hubbard. The small cabin was located on the slope of the east side of Olean Road facing the sunset, about 4 miles from the village of East Aurora. At the time of this photograph, the property was part of the Adams family farm. A small bit of the foundation still exists.

Built by the Roycrofters, this pavilion was a gift to the community. It is located two blocks south of the Roycroft Inn, in Hamlin Park, where many events took place. One of the most notable events was the memorial service held for Elbert and Alice in July 1915. For more than 60 years, it has been home to the Aurora Players theater guild.

"Brud's" House, built by Roycroft Boys

This postcard features another special Roycroft log house, Bert's House, built by the Roycroft Boys. Bert (Elbert Hubbard II) and his bride, Alta Fattey, moved in on October 12, 1904. It has been added to over the years, and the site now includes a tennis court and swimming pool. The house is located a block or so north of the Roycroft Inn on North Grove and Ridge.

Four farms supported the Roycroft Inn and community. This is a view of harvest time at the Roycroft Farm. Roycrofters and guests were enlisted to help at this time of year. The colored photo shows Elbert holding the horses, with Alice on the hay wagon and Miriam with her horse, "Asbestos," to the left. The car may be a Thomas Flyer; the Roycroft chauffeur is unidentified.

Built c. 1906, Emerson Hall was located on Prospect Street, two blocks south of the Roycroft Inn. It was built as an addition to an existing house, with a large stable and barn in the rear. There was a ballroom on the third floor. The hall served as an ancillary hotel with 30 rooms furnished in Roycroft furniture.

Six large tables seating 12 people filled the dining room of Emerson Hall. One of these signed ash Roycroft tables is in our art gallery and another is at the Roycroft Inn. The lamps and lighting fixtures were designed by Dard Hunter and are in museum and private collections throughout the United States. The lamps were wired through two holes in each table.

Emerson Hall also had a Reception Room where guests could read, write, and play the piano. Often, large groups such as bands were housed here. The building was also the dormitory for the School of Life for Boys and, later, for girls as well. The Hubbards' horses were kept at the barn here after the stable behind the inn became the Roycroft Inn laundry and staff quarters.

Photographed during the Roycrofters' heyday (c. 1913), this view is looking west on Main Street in the village of East Aurora from the railroad tracks. Here we can see the celebration flags during the Fourth of July week-long Roycroft Convention. The three-story Odd Fellows Hall (far right) is one of the few remaining buildings.

Plumbing supplies make up this float for a c. 1913 Independence Day parade. Sommer & Co. Hardware displayed the newest fashions in oak and porcelain toilets, claw-foot tubs, and decorated cast-iron cookstoves. Their store (background) was located on the south side of Main Street next door to the Globe Hotel, which is still standing.

The latest in Cleveland bicycles decorates the one-horse float of the Aurora Cycle Company. This business also located on Main Street, next door to the C. Lamb Jewelry Store.

In this Christmas greeting sent in 1929 from Bert and Alta Hubbard, we see Hubbard Hill in the making. The Hubbards' beautiful English Tudor-style home was elegantly decorated with Roycroft furnishings. The linen-fold dining room was carved by Charles Hall.

Samuel Warner's design for Elbert Hubbard's book plate shows an early style of Arts & Crafts printing. Nothing was too small to print on the hand-letter press or too insignificant to market. This bookplate is an homage to the book, the main product from 1895 until they disbanded in 1938. Showing a medieval Gothic design, the bookplate resembles bookends and is a subtle hint that Hubbard was a Gemini; his birthday is June 19.

Beautiful books printed on letter presses on handmade paper and bound with marble paper boards were also stamped with gold and had gold leaf edges. The art of the book was perfected at Roycroft when master craftsman Louis Kinder was hired in the late 1890s. Men and women under his guidance produced some of the most artistic books in the United States. These bindings are highly sought after by collectors all over the world.

The latest in Cleveland bicycles decorates the one-horse float of the Aurora Cycle Company. This business also located on Main Street, next door to the C. Lamb Jewelry Store.

In this Christmas greeting sent in 1929 from Bert and Alta Hubbard, we see Hubbard Hill in the making. The Hubbards' beautiful English Tudor-style home was elegantly decorated with Roycroft furnishings. The linen-fold dining room was carved by Charles Hall.

Alexis Jean Fournier is shown here on the right in his wonderful hollyhock, flower, and vegetable garden. The view looks south at his "Bunglehouse" and second studio on Walnut Street in East Aurora. Note the skylight in the paint shop building to the left. This 1920 photograph is signed, but the other man is unidentified. A similar view, entitled *Hollyhocks in the Garden—The Bunglehouse*, was painted in oil by Fournier and featured on the cover of *Christies* in September 1992. The painting sold for a record price at the time.

This is a close-up view of the "Bunglehouse" front door. The structure, once a chicken coop, was converted by Fournier for additional studio space. Alex Fournier and his third wife, Coral, lived here at the time of his death in 1948. Fournier also referred to the charming structure as "Les Pommier," meaning "house of the apple tree," because an apple tree was deliberately incorporated into the porch roof. This photo dates from the late 1920s or early 1930s.

Six
Objects Made by Roycrofters

The idea of making fine books as works of art is different from printing magazines full of social ideas about lifestyle changes and attitudes, but Elbert Hubbard did both with his Roycroft Press. Roycroft books sold for as much as a car or a piece of land. The press could satisfy 225,000 *Philistine* subscribers month after month. The publishing and printing were always the main crafts at Roycroft, but others were soon a viable part of the operation. Even the furniture reflected that truth with the Elbert Hubbard motto, "The Library is the first of all rooms." Bookcases, library tables, Morris chairs, and magazine stands were the mainstays of furniture production. Perhaps the furniture shop, with its ups and downs and its near closing by 1923, was alone in its marginal efforts. The other departments were profitable. The blacksmith shop produced andirons as well as hardware as early as 1898. The copper shop replaced the early blacksmith shop by 1909 as it began to produce some of the most attractive, functional quality products. Bookends and desk sets were produced first but the products soon expanded to include trays, vases, candlesticks, and bowls. Eventually, the Roycrofters made the fabulous lighting fixtures for the Roycroft Inn, Chapel, and their own Metal Arts shop. These lighting pieces were included in the Roycroft Copper Shop's catalogue and marketed everywhere. The operation was very successful. Most of the leatherwork, which was an outgrowth of producing fine bindings, was done in the furniture shop. Table mats and purses were made in the method known as modeled leather. A special process was developed for molding over forms and back filling with a composition of ground leather and glue that held the designs in place.

These objects were sold at Roycroft through book, furniture, and metal catalogs, and soon were available through more than 200 stores that featured a Roycroft department. Stores as large as Lord & Tayor, Neiman Marcus, Marshall Field, and Hengerers in Buffalo had such departments, much as Ralph Lauren's Polo line does today. Smaller stores also carried Roycroft goods; stores as far away as North Yacama, Washington, and as prestigious as the Cornell Book Store were prosperous avenues to sell Roycroft wares.

Samuel Warner's design for Elbert Hubbard's book plate shows an early style of Arts & Crafts printing. Nothing was too small to print on the hand-letter press or too insignificant to market. This bookplate is an homage to the book, the main product from 1895 until they disbanded in 1938. Showing a medieval Gothic design, the bookplate resembles bookends and is a subtle hint that Hubbard was a Gemini; his birthday is June 19.

Beautiful books printed on letter presses on handmade paper and bound with marble paper boards were also stamped with gold and had gold leaf edges. The art of the book was perfected at Roycroft when master craftsman Louis Kinder was hired in the late 1890s. Men and women under his guidance produced some of the most artistic books in the United States. These bindings are highly sought after by collectors all over the world.

Roycroft developed the technique of modeled leather book binding. Frederick Kranz was the foremost designer of this style. These bindings, which look like hand-carved wood or repousse copper, were offered at an additional $10 to $200 per book at a time when some cars cost $200. This particular binding is for one of the 20-volume sets of Elbert Hubbard's complete writings, which were produced from 1908 to 1915, just after Hubbard's death. Shown here is Volume #6, published in 1909.

In addition to books, the promotion of Roycroft products was done by catalogs that were printed and sold by the Roycrofters in an Arts & Crafts trend of the day. This 1908 furniture catalog includes 38 pages of different items; the cover was designed by Dard Hunter. Catalogs are as equally collectible as the items within.

The tall, ladder-like pyramidal magazine pedestal (left) was the Roycroft Furniture Shop's best seller. It held a year's subscription of five different-sized periodicals. Like all Roycroft furniture, it is clearly marked with the Roycroft orb or the word Roycroft. Some of these quartersawn oak pedestals are also carved with an acanthus leaf. Roycroft furniture exemplified the Arts & Crafts aesthetic by using honest construction techniques like exposed mortise and tenon joinery. This photo is from 1900.

The hall chair (right), available in oak or mahogany, was found throughout the early Roycroft buildings. A massive medieval design, it weighs more than 40 pounds. It is signed with a large Roycroft orb on the back of the center slat. One can be seen in the Elbert Hubbard/Roycroft Museum in East Aurora. It stands over 4 feet tall.

Less than two dozen men worked in the Roycroft Furniture Shop, except during times of large commissions (the Roycroft Inn in 1903 and the Grove Park Inn in 1912). Most items related to books—library tables, book cases, desks, and comfortable seating like Morris chairs. Workers at the shop made bedroom furniture for the Roycroft Inn, but these pieces were rarely for sale. A piece like this is still in the Hubbard family. Notice the Mackmurdo feet, named after Arthur Mackmurdo, the founder of the English "Century Guild."

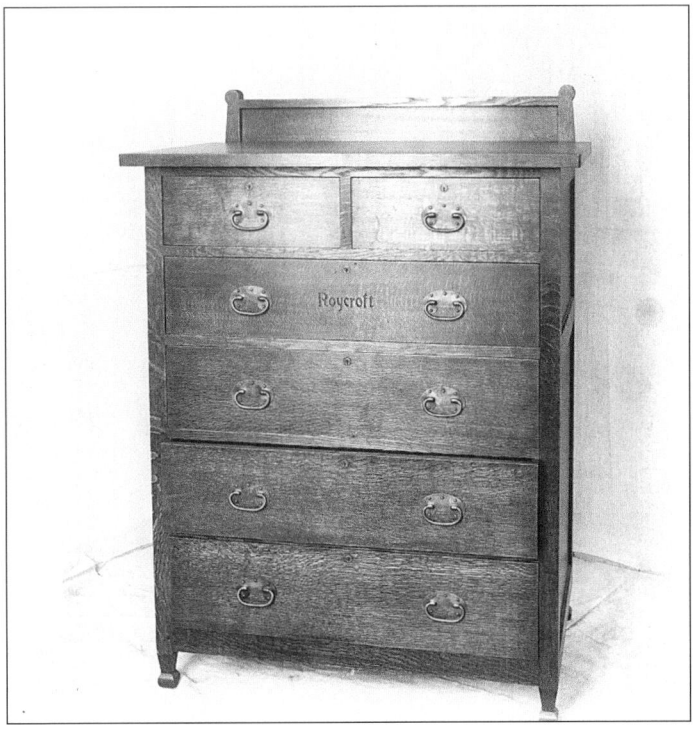

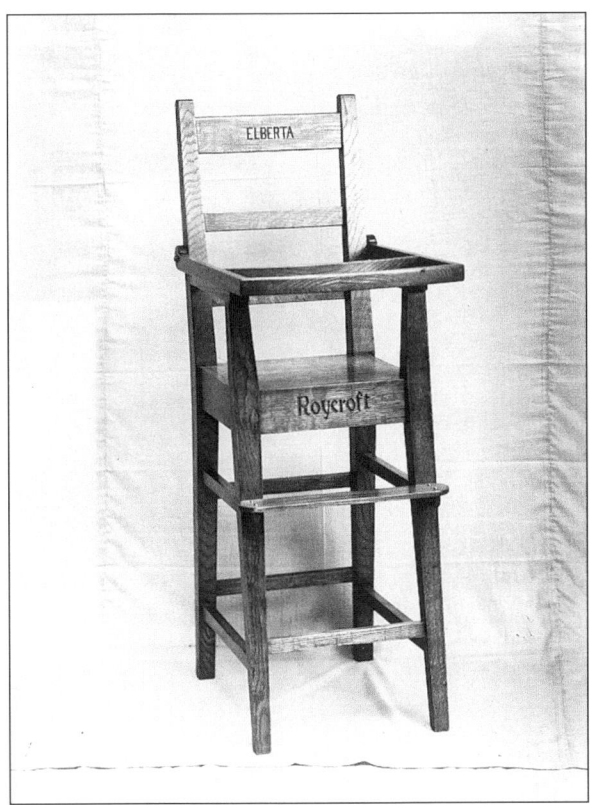

Children's Roycroft furniture was also available. This high chair has the name of Elbert Hubbard's second granddaughter, Elberta, carved into the top rail. The additional decoration was added at no charge on high chairs, children's arm chairs, rockers, and cribs. The most famous high chair belonged to Lady Bird Johnson and is in the Johnson Museum and Library in Texas. Her family could have purchased it on a visit to the Roycroft Campus, through a Roycroft catalog, or from Neiman Marcus, one of the many stores with Roycroft departments.

A few very elaborate, one-of-a-kind pieces were made at Roycroft, including the screen in this photo. It was offered for sale c. 1904, and the carving was executed by John Godsoe. The gilded and carved-leather Art Nouveau panels are the work of Frederic Kranz. The names on the top rail are those of the founding fathers of the Arts & Crafts Movement: Ruskin, Morris, Burne-Jones, and Rossetti. This piece was offered at $250 and was sold. It turned up in a New Jersey barn in the 1970s without the leather but otherwise in excellent condition. It is now the centerpiece of a major East Aurora collection. We are always glad to see pieces of furniture return home.

Victor Toothacher's 1913 concept drawing of a Roycroft interior features Roycroft andirons, candlesticks, sconces, rugs, coal buckets, leather mats, ashtrays, a large copper and mica lamp, a pedestal table, and a leather upholstered Morris chair. Roycroft made items for a complete Arts & Crafts or mission-style room. Toothacher sketched similar interiors for Gustav Stickley's magazine *The Craftsman* in 1910–1911. He was the Roycroft's master metal craftsman in charge of the Grove Park Inn commission in 1912–1913, the largest job the Roycrofters ever had.

This Arts & Crafts-period log cabin interior is fitted out in the height of "Roycroftie" style. Many similarities exist between this room and its inspiration, the Roycroft Inn library and reception rooms. Two very rare, signed double Morris chairs and two single Morris chairs surround a stone fireplace, which is flanked by murals. Tribal rugs and even a Roycroft book are in the picture. This is a *c.* 1920 view of "Sagamore Lodge," the home of Mr. & Mrs. P.B. Hanks of Wellsville, New York.

By 1914, the Roycroft had already developed small departments in shops and stores from coast to coast, from Spokane, Washington, to Los Angeles and from New Orleans to Toronto, Canada. All had similar displays, such as this view of the Corner Bookstore in Ithaca, New York, home of Cornell University (where Elbert's second son, Ralph, attended college).

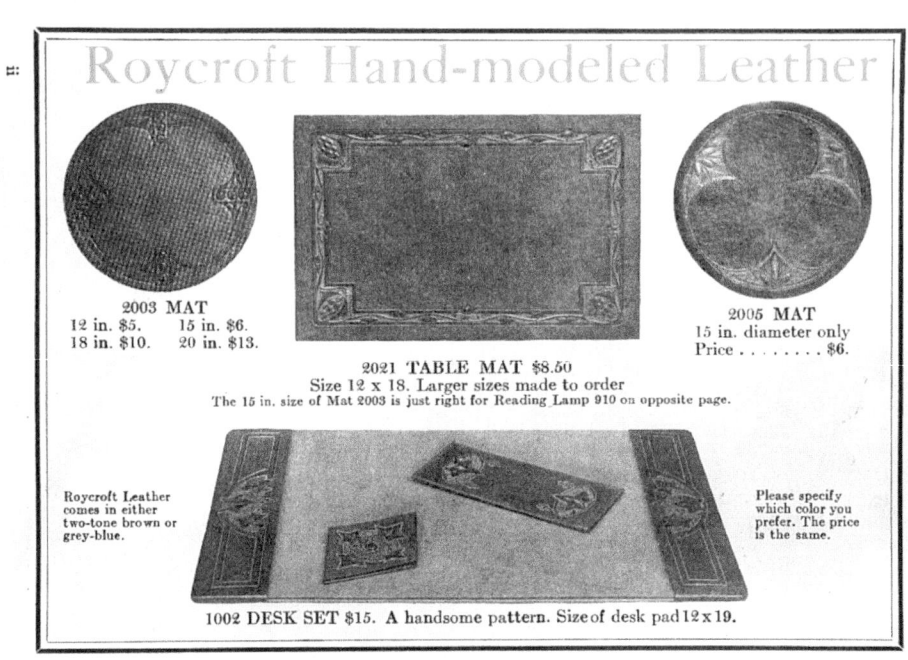

A page from a 1917 Roycroft magazine advertises their own hand-hammered and hand-modeled leather products.

During the mid-1920s, the typographers at Roycroft devised many modern designs to compete with greeting card companies of the day, including Rust-Craft and Hallmark. Roycroft cards today are a rare find for collectors. Note the early use of the word Xmas.

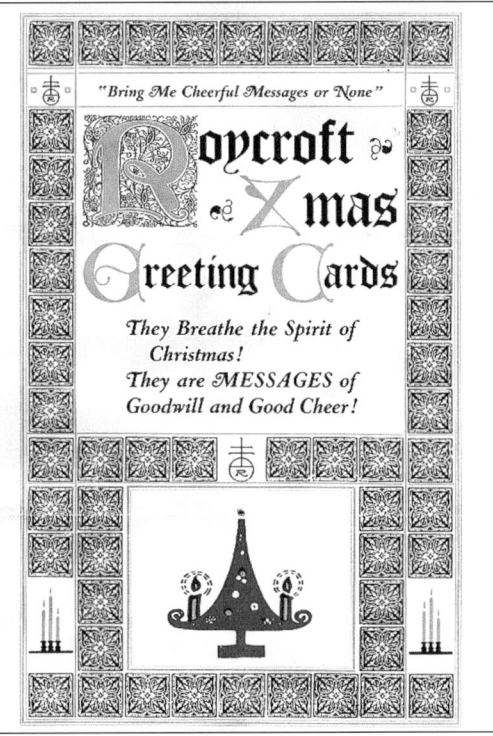

A one-of-a-kind piece, this is the Great Hall clock from the Roycroft commission for the Grove Park Inn (GPI) in Asheville, North Carolina. Begun in 1912 and finished one year later, GPI kept the Roycroft Shops humming, creating over 700 lighting fixtures and lamps and 700 or more furniture pieces for the public spaces. Two different clocks are known to have been made; this example is over 7 feet high. It still occupies a prominent place in the massive stone building's Great Hall, which has fireplaces on either side. In 1995, for the 100th anniversary of the Roycroft, the Stickley Company was licensed to make 50 limited-edition replicas; they were all sold within the year.

This postcard bears the caption, "Contented Cows, Roycroft Dairy, East Aurora." Postcards were used to promote every aspect of the Roycroft, including the products and produce from the four Roycroft farms. They made cheeses and raised potatoes that were packed in signed wooden "goodie boxes," along with hams, candies, and other items. These gift boxes were sold in Roycroft magazine ads and catalogs.

This was the quintessential Roycroft lighting fixture designed by Dard Hunter c. 1910. The piece may very well be a marriage, as the four outer lanterns were added to the original years later. Certainly the center section was executed first. Three sides represent the printer, architecture, and artist. The fourth side is made up of squares of green glass in varying shades, as are the four surrounding rectilinear lanterns, indicating that it was situated so there was little view of the back. We believe it was made that way for the entrance or foyer to the Music Salon at the south end of the peristyle doorway. For 40 years, it hung on the porch (peristyle) in front of the north entrance to the Roycroft Inn. It has been completely restored and has traveled with the Head, Heart, & Hand exhibition. It is also featured in the companion catalog. The fixture now hangs in the library dining room of the restored Roycroft Inn.

Seven
THE ROYCROFT RENAISSANCE

A Roycroft Renaissance has been in progress for nearly three decades. It is concurrent with an international Arts & Crafts revival. In 1971, the Turgeon family purchased the closed Roycroft Inn. With a great deal of enthusiasm, a wonderful relationship with Nancy Hubbard Brady, and a minimum budget, the Roycroft Inn was transformed from white woodwork, red flocked wallpaper, wagon-wheel light fixtures, and a piano bar, into a semblance of its original state. Today, the Roycroft Inn has had an $8-million restoration and features 22 suites and a guest house.

While it has been uphill all the way, the progress since 1971 began by convincing the Hubbards and other Roycroft families to loan pieces to the Arts & Crafts Movement in America exhibition in 1972. The Roycroft Inn reached National Historic Landmark status in 1986, and in 1995, it was was restored and reopened by the Margaret Wendt Foundation. In 1976, Nancy Hubbard Brady, Charles Hamilton, Rix Jennings, and Kitty Turgeon (author) founded the Roycrofters-at-Large Association (RALA). This group is still devoted to the Roycroft Campus and is restoring the "Appian Way." Their *Little Journeys* lecture series, held each spring, covers Arts & Crafts history. The organization provides a winter/holiday craft show the first weekend in December, and their reenactment of the original Roycroft Convention has become the Roycroft Summer Festival, held in June, when they also sponsor a chamber music festival. We are still very involved with the new Roycrofters.

The Aurora Historical Society expanded its Roycroft collection when they were given the house that was the home of Roycroft leather worker George ScheideMantel and his wife, Gladys, in 1985. It is now the Hubbard/Roycroft Museum House and is open several days a week, June through October. Much of the campus is still in transition. The Roycroft Inn is restored and the Roycroft Shops, although not as they were, are as Hubbard might have them today. Antique shops, an art gallery, and the "new" Roycroft potter, Janice McDuffie, have been in residence in the original furniture shop for more than 20 years. The old copper shop has incorporated several shops under one roof, including an art gallery, gift shop, an Arts & Crafts home furnishings department, and a working, teaching print shop and museum.

The Foundation for the Study of the Arts & Crafts (A&C) Movement at Roycroft, or the "Foundation at Roycroft," resides on the campus, inside the old copper shop. They manage the printing museum on the Roycroft Campus as well as sponsor A&C Elderhostels, two symposiums (one at Roycroft and a second in California), and a four-day course on A&C history at Chautauqua. Under the auspices of the foundation, lectures are given nationwide. Its presence is prominent at many A&C events and the members have an active schedule and chapter in western New York. The authors of this book are executive director and curator of the foundation.

After the Roycrofters went bankrupt in 1938, the entire Roycroft campus was purchased by Samuel Guard, shown here in his office at the Roycroft Print Shop. He came from Indiana, where he was the well-known editor of the *Breeder's Gazette*. He hoped to become Elbert Hubbard's successor. In the process of his reorganization, he leased the Roycroft Inn to Anthony A. Rohrer and the copper shop to Carl Taggarsell, who continued that shop as Roycroft Products. Taggarsell used the Roycroft mark on his items for sale and bought the building when Guard declared bankruptcy in 1941, after only two years of business. Roycroft Products never went into receivership. The bank took over the Roycroft Inn and leased it to Rohrer, who ran it through the summer of 1940; Louis Fuchs, a bank employee, then ran it until 1950, when it was sold to Edwin Miller. Miller ran it successfully for a decade.

The charming and quaint Roycroft Copper Shop, which became Roycroft Products, was sold to Eva and Roswell Strong in 1955. They continued to make Roycroft items for sale using the Roycroft name and mark; they hired ex-Roycrofters to make jewelry and other items and called their business the "Roycroft Gift Shop." They ran it successfully until the late 1960s, when it was sold to Warren Moffett, who ran it as a gift shop until 1975. The business and building were sold to this author in June 1976. We have restored the front room to the way it was, as Elbert Hubbard's bank, and remodeled the rest to have a total of three shops under one roof, including an art gallery and Roycroft Associates, an Arts and Crafts home furnishings department. Almost impossible to identify in this view are two Karl Kipp lamps, seen on either side of the front door. In May 1975 they were sold to the High Museum in Atlanta, Georgia, where they remain on display.

When the Turgeons first bought the Roycroft Inn in 1971, it had become a sorry sight. Under two operations leased to John Gephardt (1965) and Vincent Holland (1970), both of whom went bankrupt, the interior had lost its original beauty, as you can see in this picture.

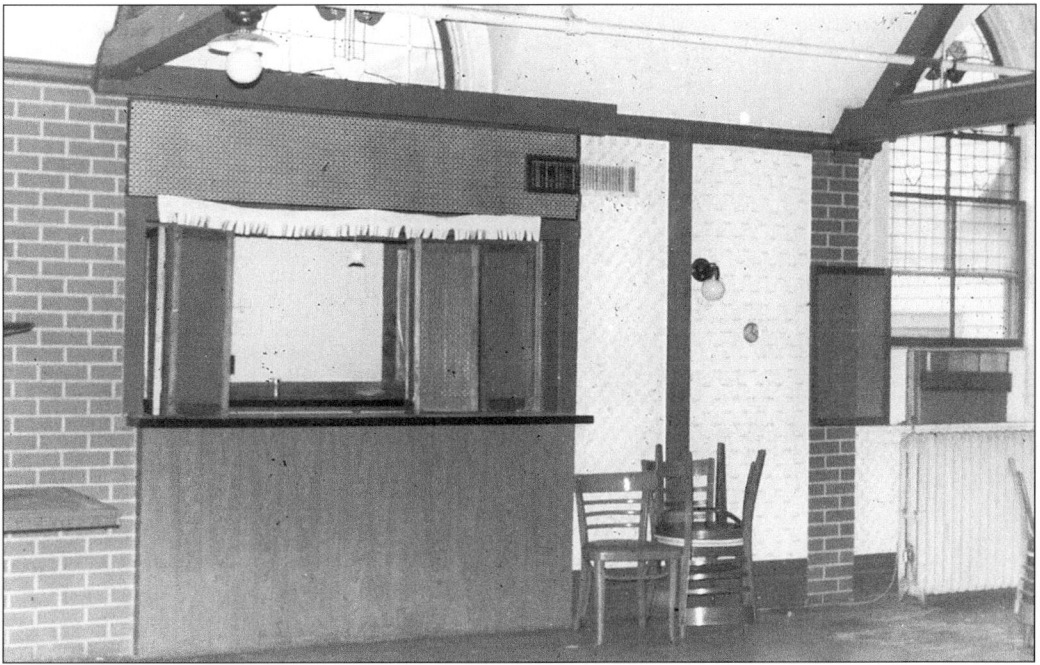

Hubbard Hall was tired and tawdry in 1971 when the Turgeons removed some of the decorative additions in order to reflect the original beauty of the room. While a vast improvement was made, it was not until 1995, after the Wendt Foundation gave the Roycroft Inn a major $8-million "face lift," that a renewed, almost-better-than-ever Roycroft Inn would appear.

Before the restoration of the John Ruskin Room, the ceiling had been dropped and everything was covered with beaver board, probably an attempt at both insulation and modernization during the 1930s. The author's collection clutters the space during restoration. From the 1930s through the 1960s, the room functioned as an apartment.

In 1976, just in time for the U.S. bicentennial, the Ruskin Room was restored as a museum. Preservation techniques were just evolving, and this room reflects a new approach to interpretive museum display. The room is no longer open to the public since the recent 1995 restoration. Those furnishings are on display at Roycroft Shops. An early book described the room as being serene and yet majestic, with green velvet curtains. It was, after all, the most prominent and luxurious of guest rooms, featuring a private bath, fireplace, and vaulted ceiling.

Shown here is a birthday celebration for the author, Kitty Turgeon, in 1976. Many of these people were on the first RALA Board of Directors. They are, from left to right, as follows: Egil Finsted, owner of the Special Guest House (then the Roycroft Handweavers); Kitty Turgeon, owner of the Roycroft Inn and Gift Shop; Chester Dylewski, owner of the original furniture shop (Roycroft Antiques); Robert Mertz, antique dealer; Linda Falkosky (Elbert Hubbard's great-granddaughter); Bonnie and Bill Todoroff, managers of the Roycroft Gift Shop; Jan Thompson, Kitty's administrative assistant; Bruce Clark, jeweler; and Michael Barrett, Roycroft Inn manager.

This is a view of the newly renovated Roycroft Shop that appeared in a Country Inn series by *Architectural Digest*.

Chester Dylewski is seen here on the peristyle of the Roycroft Inn. Early Roycroft Convention Revivals (1976–1980) had antique shows here. Dylewski and his wife, Onda, bought the original furniture shop in 1972 and have run a successful antique business with several dealers as tenants in that building for more than 25 years.

In December 1977, the Burchfield Art Center in Buffalo, New York, sponsored the second Roycroft exhibition, *The Roycroft Movement: Spirit for Today*. (The first was at the Erie Art Museum in 1974.) It was accompanied by lectures and a panel discussion as seen here. Pictured from left to right are Emil Sahlin (one of the original Roycroft printers), Miriam Hubbard Roelofs (Elbert and Alice's only child, seen here in her mid-80s), and Robert Volz (rare books custodian from Williams College).

This picture of Jay Nicely in 1979 was taken at the fourth Roycroft Renaissance Convention dinner. At the time, he was vice president of the short-lived Elbert Hubbard Foundation, which was absorbed by the RALA in 1981. Author Kitty Turgeon served as president of the RALA from 1978 to 1980.

During the Roycroft Renaissance Convention weekend in 1981, the original furniture shop was almost destroyed by fire. Fortunately, only the third floor is gone; the rest has been rebuilt. It has housed Roycroft Antiques, various antique shops, an art gallery, and the Roycroft Potters since the mid-1970s.

This April 1981 photo shows the third-floor room labeled "Corot" at the Roycroft Inn. The image was taken for the Historic House Association Collection of wallpapers that was released in 1982. In 1988, the paper was discontinued and the exclusive rights were sold to Roycroft Shops. It is still sold today and is also available as a border. It is important to note that this was never historic Roycroft paper. It was inspired and adapted in 1981 from the Roycroft china designed in 1905.

A year later, in September 1982, the authors of this book took over the Roycroft Inn as its new innkeepers. Our most important contribution has been the incredible process of making 14 of the original Roycroft buildings National Historic Landmarks. It was this designation that brought the Roycroft to the attention of the National Trust, the village of East Aurora, and the Wendt Foundation.

The Roycroft Renaissance sculpture, created in 1984, stands proud with the Roycroft Print Shop (now the Cornell Extension Center) in the background. The RALA gifted this piece to the town of Aurora (now located in the original chapel), where it adorns their lawn on Main Street. The sculpture's design and construction was donated by Paul Boccolucci, sculptor and Roycroft Renaissance artisan. The material was donated by a local company; ironically, it is rejected torpedo steel! The utility and installation costs were raised by the RALA with one of the most elegant dinners the Roycroft Inn has ever hosted. It is a tribute to a new era; at night it is astonishingly visible and with its proper lighting announces: "Roycroft is Here!"

At one of the annual Roycroft "Applefests" in October 1984, Congressman Jack Kemp cut the cake. It was that day that he agreed to help Turgeon and Rust obtain National Historic Landmark status for the 14 buildings of the Roycroft Campus. In the 1960s, when Kemp played for the Buffalo Bills, the team had a training table and stayed at the Roycroft Inn while practicing at the Knox Polo Field. Kemp knew and appreciated the building and was an enormous help in securing the designation, which was official in March 1986. From left to right are Tom Reyolds (then county representative), Kitty Turgeon (innkeeper), Jack Kemp, and Robert Rust (general manager). The woman, a local Republican leader, is unidentified.

In 1986, on her 100th birthday, Gladys ScheideMantel gave the home she and her husband George, a master leather craftsman, had built for them in 1910 to the Aurora Historical Society. The house was constructed by the Roycroft building team. It is now the Hubbard/Roycroft Museum and houses an extensive collection of Roycroft that was owned by the ScheideMantel's. The gift, given by the Godfrey family, constitutes more than one-half of the museum house holdings. The house is listed on the National Register of Historic Places and has extensive period gardens maintained by the local "master gardeners." It is open June through October, Wednesday, Saturday, and Sunday afternoons, or by appointment.

The Alex Fournier House, photographed in 1987, is the home of authors Turgeon and Rust. The house is painted in appropriate colors from the Roycroft Palette (which was developed by the authors and the Sherwin Williams Paint Company). It is available in stores as 16 interior and 16 exterior Arts & Crafts colors.

The value of Roycroft furniture has gone up so much that, by 1986, the Roycroft Shops had created a line of reproductions and reissues made by Roycroft Renaissance artisans and Buffalo China called "the Roycroft Collection." This photo was taken at the Fournier House in 1992. Today, several pieces are licensed by Roycroft Shops and made by the L.&J.G. Stickley Co., including both of the magazine stands. Unique pieces are still made by local craftsmen.

Mary Roelofs Stott, the eldest granddaughter of Elbert and Alice Hubbard, was a writer and musician. In the early 1990s, she read her poetry and talked about the grandfather she never met. He was the inspiration for her book, *Rebel With Reverence*, which is now in its third edition.

In the mid-1980s, the Roycroft Shops expanded to include an art gallery and home furnishings department as well as the Roycroft Gift Shop. The three were renamed Roycroft Shops, Inc. In 1994, at the age of 89, Rix Jennings designed and made the sign shown in this c. 1997 photo.

The master craftsmen in this 1992 photo are, from left to right, cofounder of RALA and artist Rix Jennings, jeweler and metalsmith Alburn Sleeper, and cabinetmaker Tom Harris. Sleeper and Harris are past presidents of the RALA.

This dramatic view of the restored reception room of the Roycroft Inn is a favorite shot of photographers and has been seen in several magazines and books since 1995. The chandeliers and sconces are reproductions made by the Roycroft Shops.

This is a closeup of a portion of the 27-foot mural of Venice, painted in 1905 by Alexis Jean Fournier, that is the highlight of the eight murals in the Roycroft Music Salon. The murals were restored in 1996.

My Garden at Evening is a painting by Alex Fournier of his backyard, looking toward the rear of the Roycroft Furniture Shop; the Roycroft Firehouse is seen in the center. This painting was done in the early 1900s and is in the authors' collection. It has been prominent in several exhibitions including "The Wayward Muse" at the Albright-Knox Art Gallery in Buffalo in 1989 and the traveling exhibition "Head, Heart, & Hand," which originated at the Memorial Art Gallery in Rochester, New York, in 1995 and then went to seven locations coast to coast. Another exhibition, "Roycroft Desktop," which also began in 1995 from the Burchfield-Penney Art Center in Buffalo, traveled for three years and returned in 1998. A large part of it is on permanent display at the art center and is called "The Roycroft Legacy." The 100th anniversary of Roycroft and the reopening of the Roycroft Inn, along with these shows, has focused a great deal of attention on Roycroft.

RALA board members pose during the installation of the National Historic Landmark Plaque and garden in front of the Roycroft Shops in 1990. They are, from left to right, as follows: (front) Jim Williams, Robert Rust, and Grace Meibohm Demme; (standing) then President William Hartung, Sean McAtee, Greg Engle, Tom Bojanowski, Onda Dylewski, Kitty Turgeon, and Bruce Bland.